UNDONE

*A Modern
Rendering of*
**JOHN DONNE'S
DEVOTIONS**

PHILIP YANCEY

UNDONE: A Modern Rendering of John Donne's *Devotions*
©2023 Philip Yancey

RABBIT ROOM PRESS
3321 Stephens Hill Lane
Nashville, TN 37013
info@rabbitroom.com

ISBN 9781951872175

All scripture quotations, unless otherwise indicated, are taken from the Holy Bible, New International Version®, NIV®. Copyright ©1973, 1978, 1984, 2011 by Biblica, Inc.™ Used by permission. All rights reserved worldwide. (In some cases, italicized scripture in the paraphrased chapters follow John Donne's paraphrase.)

An earlier version of this material was published as *A Companion in Crisis* (2021). Some of the commentary under Day 1-2 and 26-30 has been adapted from the booklet *Devotions by John Donne* ©2020 by The Trinity Forum and from the book *Soul Survivor* ©2001 by SCCT and published by Doubleday, a division of Penguin Random House, LLC. Used by permission. All rights reserved worldwide.

For bulk purchases and reprint permission contact info@rabbitroom.com.

Except there were some light, there could be no shadow.
—JOHN DONNE

CONTENTS

PREFACE

Day 1   A Way through Crisis
Day 2   What to Make of It?

JOHN DONNE'S
DEVOTIONS
A Modern Rendering

Day 3   Early Symptoms
Day 4   Faltering Senses
Day 5   Bedridden
Day 6   Calling the Doctor
Day 7   Quarantine
Day 8   Fear
Day 9   Consultation
Day 10   The King's Physician
Day 11   Diagnosis
Day 12   Stealth Symptoms
Day 13   The Heart

Day 14   Breath

Day 15   A Rash

Day 16   Critical Days

Day 17   Insomnia

Day 18   The Funeral Bell

Day 19   The "Passing" Bell

Day 20   The Death Knell

Day 21   Hope

Day 22   Purging

Day 23   Resurrection

Day 24   The Source

Day 25   Relapse

Day 26   Death Defanged

Day 27   The Peace of Acceptance

Day 28   Finding Meaning in Suffering

Day 29   Compassion, Not Blame

Day 30   From Fear to Trust

PREFACE

I WAS BORN AT THE HEIGHT OF AN EPIDEMIC. In 1949, just over 42,000 Americans contracted the disease polio, most of them under the age of five. Less than 10 percent of the afflicted died, but a large number experienced paralysis. Children with crutches, leg braces, and deformed limbs were a commonplace sight, spreading fear among parents and children alike. My father, though an adult, somehow became infected. He spent several months in an iron lung, completely paralyzed, and then died at age 23.

My first book explored the question *Where Is God When It Hurts?*, a question that had hung over my brother and me like the shadow of a missing father. In the years since, my writing has often circled around the issues raised by pain and suffering. Then came 2020, when a global health crisis put everyone on the planet at risk. Within weeks, a tiny virus overwhelmed hospitals, disrupted economies, and upended everyday social interactions. For a time, everything came undone.

We had no instruction manual on how to respond to a pandemic—or did we? Historians soon dug up lessons from prior outbreaks of diseases such as polio, smallpox, cholera, bubonic plague, and Spanish influenza. At various times, these scourges spread terror and brought normal life to a halt. Each pandemic reduced humans to frail, bewildered creatures facing questions that seemed to have no satisfying answers.

Where could I find a guide who had survived such an ordeal, and who offered wisdom for the ages? I found the answer in a journal predating COVID-19 by four centuries. John Donne wrote *Devotions upon Emergent Occasions* in 1623, during a bubonic plague epidemic in his city of London. Here, at last, was a master tutor, a trustworthy companion in crisis.

Thrilled at the discovery, I sequestered myself in a mountain retreat and began a project that would occupy me for several months. My goal: to make more accessible for 21st-century readers the timeless insights from one of our greatest writers. The understanding and treatment of disease has changed dramatically since Donne's time, and yet I know of no better account of someone confronting God during a health crisis.

Ironically, just as this book was being edited, my doctor confirmed a most unwelcome diagnosis: 'Philip, you have Parkinson's Disease," she said. Suddenly I knew exactly how Donne felt when he wrote the first words of his book: "Variable, and therefore miserable condition of man! this minute I was well, and am ill, this minute." Unlike Donne's feverish battle with immediate symptoms, I face the challenge of adapting to a chronic, degenerative disease. Yet I am finding that his journal of suffering points the way toward a hard-won faith.

John Donne composed twenty-three meditations charting the stages of his illness. They include some of the most famous passages in English literature: "No man is an island . . . never send to know for whom the bell tolls; it tolls for thee. . . ." To Donne's meditations I have added seven entries that explain some of the author's background. Donne wrote as a form of contemplation, and his reflections should be read that way. I recommend reading one entry per day over a thirty-day period, slowly and meditatively.

I was brutally selective as I edited *Devotions*, slashing anything that required explanations: archaic science or Greek mythology, or even obscure Bible passages. I retained only parts that seem to have an immediate relevance, not only to the COVID-19 crisis, but to any crisis that stirs up existential questions. And, wincing at my own effrontery, I sought to tame his complicated writing style into something that modern readers can more readily absorb.

I sought to extract from Donne's literary masterpiece universal truths on how to live and how to die. In this version, you will miss many of Donne's alliterations, puns, and rhetorical devices. If you find yourself bothered by my rendering, or simply curious about what's missing, well, I encourage you to download the original (available free: https://freeditorial. com/en/books/devotions-upon-emergent-occasions).

I give special thanks to Doubleday and Waterbrook, the publishers of my book *Soul Survivor*, from which I drew some of my commentary. My literary agent, Kathryn Helmers, was most helpful in conceiving this project, and my executive assistant, Joannie Degnan Barth, was invaluable throughout the process. Selections were published in a booklet by The Trinity Forum and also self-published under the title *A Companion in Crisis*.

A Way Through Crisis

(Philip Yancey)

The words leaped out at me from the very first page of John Donne's *Devotions upon Emergent Occasions*, when I came across it in my twenties. I had known Donne's reputation as one of England's greatest poets, but nothing had prepared me for his raw account of confrontations with God during a personal crisis.

In early seventeenth-century London, Donne held one of the most eminent religious positions of the time, Dean of St. Paul's Cathedral. In the midst of a deadly pandemic, he was straining to give pastoral comfort to his parishioners. The city's population had been decimated, and funeral bells relentlessly tolled every day. Donne felt spiritually drained and helpless. Then the first symptoms of illness appeared on his own body, which to his doctors seemed a clear sign of the bubonic plague. For a month he lay sick, hearing the church bell toll for others and wondering if his death would be the next announced.

Though severely weakened by illness, Donne drew upon his writer's instinct and managed to chronicle each stage. *What are you trying to tell us, God? How could you strike me down when my flock needs me so desperately? In my youth I was a sexual profligate—is this your way of cruelly nailing me to my bed? Do you enjoy watching us humans writhe in pain? Do you still heal people? What message are you trying to get across to the world?* He agonized over questions like these, and scoured his memory of the Bible for insights and answers.

"O God, my God": following in the tradition of Job and Augustine, Donne wrote his book in the second person, addressing God directly. In style, *Devotions* differs from his stately sermons, or his playful, witty poetry. His meditations are personal, heated, moody, bordering on unstable. They reflect the feverish state of a self-absorbed writer pushed to the brink.

As he writes, Donne's spiritual outlook wavers between sublime trust and paranoia. In today's term, he uses a passive-aggressive approach with God: now demanding, now shyly retreating. Sometimes he uses the journal as a form of cognitive therapy, talking himself into faith when he has none, and into hope when he feels only despair.

While I was sheltering in place during the early days of the COVID-19 pandemic, I turned to Donne's book again, struck by its direct application to our modern crisis. Since his time, science has changed so much as to be unrecognizable. Galileo's and Copernicus's notions of the universe were just making the rounds in his day, and the germ theory of disease was unknown. Donne's physicians treated him with bloodlettings, and applied pigeons to his head and feet to draw away vapours and humours. Yet Donne's remonstrations with God could have been written yesterday.

As I read, I saw Donne struggling with many of the same questions that would be voiced during the COVID-19 pandemic nearly four hundred years later. Claustrophobically confined to his bedroom, he let his mind roam, in search of understanding for what he was going through. I thought of our modern equivalent, of patients quarantined in ICU, their bodies treated like broken machine parts, alone except for the occasional appearance of helpers wearing masks and space suits. Ventilators and breathing tubes did not exist in Donne's day, but the crude techniques of purging and bloodletting similarly made the treatment seem worse than the disease.

What would a great writer in such circumstances produce today, especially a writer of faith? Probably something very similar to John Donne's *Devotions*. His journal of wrestling with God is timeless, applicable not only for a crisis of illness, but for any of the crises, large or small, that we moderns face on this troubled planet.

Through it all, Donne never loses his wit or his mastery of the English language. The result is such a lasting achievement that when, in 2017, the British newspaper *The Guardian* selected the one hundred best nonfiction books of all time, John Donne's *Devotions* ranked high on the list.

Over the years I have bought copies of *Devotions* and given them to friends. "Did you read it?" I've asked time and again, only to get a sheepish reply such as, "I tried, really, but just couldn't get past the language and old-fashioned syntax." Some of Donne's sentences wander through a maze of subordinate clauses and run more than two hundred words. Despite the book's rich insights, few read it today outside of an academic setting, and even scholars need a commentary to help explain his obscure allusions.

Donne published his book a mere decade after the King James Bible, which now has scores of translations and paraphrases to aid the modern reader. In an act of either daring or folly, I decided to attempt a modern rendering of this classic work on suffering.

Among other things, COVID-19 has reminded us that we are all mortal; 100 percent of us will die. Some moderns seem surprised, almost offended by the fact of death. Donne wrote at a time when death was commonplace, when half of all children died before reaching adulthood and life expectancy was thirty-three years.

Dr. Lydia Dugdale, a physician in New York on the front lines of the coronavirus pandemic, saw the crisis as a chance to recover the art of dying, or *Ars Moriendi*. People in the late Middle Ages prepared for death as an actor might prepare for a final performance. The preparations included repenting of sins, attempts to mend family ruptures, division of the will, and a gathering of loved ones for final words from the dying person. As Dugdale worked on her book (*The Lost Art of Dying: Reviving Forgotten Wisdom,* 2020), all around her COVID victims were dying alone, unable to speak, isolated from family members.

Donne's *Devotions* can be seen as a kind of prelude to death, though not in the classic *Ars Moriendi* genre. Donne accepted as a matter of fact that suffering was indeed "God's megaphone." That did not, however, stop him from shouting back. He had more the style of Dylan Thomas:

Do not go gentle into that good night,
Old age should burn and rave at close of day;
Rage, rage against the dying of the light.

John Donne burned, raved, and raged. By recording his encounters for posterity, he became a guide who can help us face our own fears and confusion in the midst of a crisis, while also finding a way through it.

2

What to Make of It?

(Philip Yancey)

No matter where I start, I usually end up writing about pain. My friends have suggested various reasons for this propensity: a deep scar from childhood, or perhaps a biochemical overdose of melancholy. I do not know. All I know is that I set out to write about something lovely, like the diaphanous wing of a mayfly, and before long I find myself back in the shadows, writing about the brief, tragic life of a mayfly.

"How can I write about anything else?" is the best explanation I can come up with. Is there a more fundamental fact of human existence? I was born in pain, squeezed out through torn and bloody tissues, and I offered up, as my first evidence of life, a wail. I will likely die in pain as well. Between those brackets of pain, I live out my days, limping from the first toward the final. As Donne's contemporary George Herbert put it, "I cried when I was born and every day shows why."

John Donne's illness was only the latest encounter in a life marked by suffering. His father had died in John's fourth year. The Catholic faith of his family proved a crippling disability in those days of Protestant persecution: Catholics could not hold office, were fined for attending Mass, and many were tortured for their beliefs. (The word "oppressed" derives from a popular torture technique: unrepentant Catholics were placed under a board on which heavy boulders were heaped to literally *press* the life out of the martyrs.) After distinguishing himself at Oxford and Cambridge, Donne was denied a degree because of his religious affiliation. His brother died in prison, serving time for having sheltered a priest.

At first, Donne responded to these difficulties by rebelling against all faith. A notorious Don Juan, he celebrated his sexual exploits in some of the most frankly erotic poems in all of English literature. Finally, riven by guilt, he renounced his promiscuous ways in favor of marriage. He had fallen under the spell of a seventeen-year-old beauty so quick and bright that she reminded him of sunlight.

In a bitter irony, just as Donne decided to settle down, his life took a calamitous turn. Anne More's father determined to punish his new son-in-law, whom he thought unsuitable. He got Donne fired from his job as secretary to a nobleman and had him, along with the minister who performed the ceremony, thrown into prison. Disconsolate, Donne wrote his pithiest poem: "John Donne, Anne Donne, Un-done."

Once released from jail, Donne, now blackballed, could not find further employment. He had lost any chance to fulfill his ambition to serve in the court of King James. For nearly a decade he and his wife lived in poverty, in a cramped house that steadily filled with their offspring, at the rate of one per year. Anne was subject to periodic depression, and more than once nearly died in childbirth. John, probably malnourished, suffered from acute headaches, intestinal cramps, and gout. His longest work during this period was an extended essay on the advantages of suicide.

Sometime during that gloomy decade, John Donne converted to the Church of England. His career blocked at every turn, he decided at the age of forty-two to seek ordination as an Anglican priest. Contemporaries gossiped about his "conversion of convenience" and scoffed that he had actually "wanted to be Ambassador to Venice, not Ambassador to God." But Donne considered it a true calling. He earned a Doctor of Divinity degree from Cambridge, promised to put aside his poetry for the sake of the priesthood, and devoted himself exclusively to parish work.

⌐

The year after Donne took his first church, Anne died. She had borne twelve children in all, five of whom died in infancy. John preached his wife's funeral sermon, choosing as his text a poignantly autobiographical passage from the book of Lamentations: "Lo, I am the man that hath seen affliction." (3:1 KJV) He made a solemn vow not to remarry, lest a stepmother bring his children further grief, which consequently meant he had to assume many household duties and use precious funds for outside help.

This, then, was the priest appointed to London's largest church, St. Paul's Cathedral, in 1621: a lifelong melancholic, tormented by guilt over the sins of his youth, failed in all his ambitions (except poetry, which he had forsworn), sullied by accusations of insincerity. He hardly seemed a likely candidate to lift a nation's spirits in plague times. Nonetheless, Donne applied himself to his new task with vigor. He refused to join the many who were evacuating London and instead stayed with his beleaguered parishioners. He arose every morning at four a.m. and studied until ten. In the era of the King James Bible and William Shakespeare, educated Londoners honored eloquence and elocution, and in these John Donne had no equal. He delivered sermons of such power that soon, despite London's declining population, the vast cathedral was crowded with worshipers.

During John Donne's time, three waves of the Great Plague swept through the city, the last epidemic alone killing forty thousand people. Those who fell ill were quarantined for twenty days, with a paper reading "Lord have mercy upon us" nailed to the door. In all, a third of London died, and another third fled to the countryside, transforming whole neighborhoods into ghost towns. Grass grew between the cobblestones. Mangy, half-crazed prophets stalked the deserted streets, crying out judgment, and in truth nearly everyone believed God had sent the plague as a scourge for London's sins. Londoners flocked to Dean Donne for an explanation, or at least a word of comfort.

And then the first spots of illness appeared on Donne's own body. It was the plague, doctors told him. He had little time left. For several weeks he lay at the threshold of death. The prescribed treatments were as vile as the illness: bleedings, toxic poultices, the application of vipers and pigeons to remove "evil vapours." During this dark time, forbidden to read or study but permitted to write, Donne carried on a no-holds-barred wrestling match with God Almighty. While lying in bed, convinced he was dying, he composed the book *Devotions*.

Some writers report that the knowledge of imminent

death produces a state of heightened concentration, somewhat like an epileptic fit; perhaps Donne felt this as he worked on his journal of illness. The writing lacks his usual tight control. The sentences, dense, strung together in free association, overladen with concepts, mirror the feverish state of Donne's mind. He wrote as though he had to pour into the words every significant thought and emotion that had ever occurred to him.

"I feel miserable! A minute ago I was well, and now I'm sick," the book begins. Anyone confined to bed for more than a few days can identify with the circumstances, trivial yet overpowering, that Donne proceeds to describe: a sleepless night, boredom, doctors in whispered consultation, the false hope of remission followed by the dread reality of relapse.

Donne pictures himself as a sailor tossed about by the towering swells of an ocean in storm: he gets an occasional glimpse of faraway land, only to lose it with the next giant wave. Other writers have described the vicissitudes of illness with similar power; what sets Donne's work apart is his intended audience: God himself. In the tradition of Job, Jeremiah, and the psalmists, Donne uses the arena of his personal trials as a staging ground for his great wrestling match with the Almighty. After spending a lifetime in confused wandering, he has finally reached a place where he can offer some service to God, and now, at that precise moment, he is struck by a deadly illness. Nothing appears on the horizon but fever, pain, and death.

What to make of it?

John Donne's
DEVOTIONS
A Modern Rendering

3

EARLY SYMPTOMS

I FEEL MISERABLE! A minute ago I was well, and now I'm sick.

This illness took me by complete surprise, and I have no idea what caused it. I follow a strict diet and get plenty of exercise, but what's the use? It's as if I worked for years to construct a sturdy house, painstakingly fitting each stone together, only to have it blown to pieces by a sudden explosion. Sickness is like that. Despite all my health precautions, it sweeps in like an intruder, battering my body and assaulting my mind.

O our miserable condition on planet earth! God may have planted a spark of immortality in us humans, but we rebelled, and now we must live out our days in death's shadow. At the first sign of illness, my fears take over. I check my pulse, examine my urine, test for fever. Could this be the beginning of my end? Anxiety seizes my mind, aggravating my symptoms and stoking my fear. Just the thought of catching this plague makes me ill.

We inhabit a planet subject to the whims of nature, which are duplicated in our own frail bodies. Storms buffet us, flashes of lightning blind us, earthquakes cause sudden trembling, our life-giving blood overflows its banks. Is this God's idea of honor, to grant us humans the awareness that at any moment suffering may strike, with one of these torments leading to our death?

What other creature has the ability to hasten its own execution by fueling sickness with apprehension on the one hand or depression on the other—as if the natural fever wouldn't destroy us fast enough on its own. What a miserable state we humans live in!

REFLECTION

IF I WERE MERELY A BODY—dust and ashes—I might protest to the Lord, who made me of this dust and will one day gather up these ashes. God's hand was the wheel upon which this clay vessel was shaped, and also the urn in which these ashes will be preserved. My dust and ashes form the temple of the Holy Spirit—could marble be more precious? Why, then, this mistreatment of my body?

But no, I am more than dust and ashes. I am also a soul, and on that grounds I bring my case before you, my God. Why isn't my soul as sensible as my body? Why doesn't my soul have the same early warnings about sin as my body feels toward illness? Why doesn't a pulse quicken in my soul at the approach of temptation, and why don't tears in my eyes alert me to spiritual sickness?

Sometimes I fight off temptation, yes, but other times I go, I run, I fly into its paths. I break into houses where the plague lives! I fall sick, bedridden, and terminally ill in the practice of sin, yet with no warning, no symptom of my sickness. I never recognize the fever of lust, of envy, of ambition, until it's too late.

In the midst of his physical suffering, your servant Job didn't incriminate you, God, so in my spiritual suffering I dare not. After all, you have imprinted a kind of pulse in our soul that beats out our spiritual condition, but we don't take the readings. That pulse is our conscience, which we all too often ignore. We rationalize it, joke it away, or drink and sleep it away—anything to silence the alarm.

Will God make a watch and leave out the spring? Will God infuse us with grace once, but not again? No, we're not abandoned. Though I may be a prodigal son, somehow God has chosen not to disown me. After distributing our portion of the inheritance and watching us squander it, God offers us still more.

We are God's tenants here and yet the landlord pays our rent—imagine! God pays us, not yearly, not quarterly, but hourly. Every minute, God extends more mercy.

PRAYER

MOST GRACIOUS GOD, because you are eternal I know you are a circle, containing first and last and all times at once. We humans, however, experience life as a direct line, leading from our beginning through all our ways to our end. Enable me, Father, by your grace, to look forward to my end; and to look backward too, recalling the free gifts you have showered on me from the beginning. By remembering your gift of planting me as a pastor in the church, and your gift long before that of writing me in the book of life—by remembering those things, Lord, may I learn to call upon your mercies now, when I need you.

Sharpen my hearing, Lord. I want my warning signals to be hair-triggered, alert to the stealthy approach of sin, so that I may retreat quickly from what in the past I greedily flew toward. To hear your voice at the beginning of a sickness, of a sin, is true health. If I can discern your light early and hear your voice, O Lord, *Then your light will break forth like the dawn, and your healing will quickly appear* (Isaiah 58:8).

I know the opposite danger as well: of an overly tender conscience, of cringing at every whiff of sin so that I hide away and avoid the world at all cost. Instead, align my conscience with your will so precisely, Lord, that I can trust you to speak to me at the beginning of every such sickness, at the approach of every sin. Assure me that if I hear that voice and run to you, you will preserve me from falling, or will raise me up again when I do indeed fall.

Do this, O Lord, for his sake, who knows our natural infirmities, for he had them, and knows the weight of our sins, for he paid a dear price for them: your Son, our Savior, Christ Jesus. Amen.

4

FALTERING SENSES

HUMAN BEINGS, SUPPOSEDLY THE NOBLEST creatures on earth, melt away like statues made not of clay or iron, but of snow. A simple fever, heat produced within our own bodies, can reduce us to a pile of dead cells. How quickly does the fever take its toll? Sooner than you can answer the question—no, sooner than you can even think of the question.

When I feel the first tramping feet of the disease's approach, I dread its victory. My senses revolt. In the twinkling of an eye, I can barely see. Instantly my taste turns insipid and bland, my appetite becomes dull and desireless. My knees buckle, my legs lack strength. At night sleep, the foreshadower of death, eludes me, making way for the original, death itself, to succeed.

As part of Adam's punishment, God declared, *By the sweat of your brow you will eat your food until you return to the ground, since from it you were taken; for dust you are and to dust you will return* (Genesis 3:19). Fever amplifies the curse. I have earned bread by the sweat of my brow, and now I sweat nonstop, from my brow to the sole of my foot, but I have no taste for bread or anything else. Miserable state of humankind, where half the world lacks food and the other half lacks the stomach for it!

REFLECTION

NO PERSON IS SO SMALL, compared to the greatest, as the greatest person is, compared to God. Consider a man who owns nothing—no, consider an enslaved person, whose very body is owned by another—and compare him to the greatest leaders in the world: that gives only a hint of what it's like for me to approach God with my voice. Nevertheless, I dare to cry out.

Trembling, I ask, "My God, my God, why have you thrown your anger so quickly upon me? Why do you melt me, scatter me, pour me like water upon the ground? What have I done to deserve this sudden attack of illness? You delayed judgment of the world for 120 years in Noah's time. You put up with a rebellious generation of Israelites for 40 years in the wilderness. Won't you suspend my sentence for one minute? Go ahead, finish me off so promptly that when some ask "How long was he sick?" they'll hear the answer, "Death pressed upon him from the first minute."

You visit us, my Lord, not in whirlwinds but in the soft and gentle breeze. You who breathed a soul into me, will your breath also blow it out? Surely it is not your hand pressing this suffering onto me—surely not you. The severing sword, the raging fire, the desert winds, and the diseases that afflicted Job came from Satan's hands, not yours.

At the same time, Lord, I know that you have led me continually with your own hand and will not correct me with someone else's. My parents would not give me over to a servant's correction, nor my God to Satan's. David, who knew your chastening, once said, *Let us fall into the hands of the*

Lord, for his mercy is great (2 Samuel 24:14).

Trusting in God's mercy, I turn my mind from the haste of this illness in dissolving my body, to the much quicker haste God will use in re-forming this dust again at the resurrection. Then I shall hear the angels proclaim, "Rise, all you dead!" Though lying in a grave, with restored hearing I'll hear that summons, and all will rise, faster than any one dies here.

PRAYER

O MOST GRACIOUS GOD, who perfects your own purposes, you reminded me by the first pang of sickness that I must die. As it continued besieging my body, you reminded me further that I may die even now. With the first symptoms you awakened me; as the disease progressed, you cast me down to call me up to yourself. By dulling my bodily senses to the pleasures of this world, you have sharpened my spiritual senses to my awareness of yourself. After stripping me of myself, you are clothing me with yourself.

As my body continues to deteriorate, O Lord, I only ask that you speed up the pace and lift my soul toward you. My taste has not vanished, but changed its desire: to sit at David's table, *to taste and see, that the Lord is good* (Psalm 34:8). My stomach has not gone, but gone up, toward the supper of the Lamb with your saints in heaven. My knees give way, but because of that I can easily kneel and fix myself upon you. *A heart at peace gives life to the body,* and a heart directed to you is a heart at peace (Proverbs 14:30).

David wrote, *"Because of your wrath there is no health in*

my body; there is no soundness in my bones because of my sin" (Psalm 38:3). Interpret for me what is happening, Lord. If you call this sickness correction, and not anger, then perhaps some health remains in my flesh. Transfer my sins, which displease you, onto him with whom you are so well pleased, Christ Jesus, and soundness will return to my bones.

O my God who appeared to Moses in a burning bush, in the midst of these brambles and thorns of sickness I ask you to appear to me. Abide close to me, even in these sharp and thorny times. Do this, O Lord, for his sake, who was no less the King of heaven for you allowing him to be crowned with thorns in this world.

5

BEDRIDDEN

HUMANS HAVE A UNIQUE ADVANTAGE: we stand erect and upright, unlike other creatures who must grovel on the ground. Heaven represents our true home, and our very posture inclines us to contemplate that place where our souls will one day rest.

How quickly we fall, though! Adam lay flat upon the ground when God breathed into him the breath of life, and when the time comes to withdraw that breath from us, we prepare by lying flat upon our beds. A fever can depose any of us, can bring down a head that wore a crown of gold yesterday to ground level today. The dictator lies as low as the people he trampled on; the judge who signs pardons is too weak to lift his hand to beg his own.

Even a cramped prison cell allows the prisoner two or three steps, or at least room enough to stand or sit and enjoy some change of posture. In contrast, a sick bed is a grave in which the head lies as low as the feet. Every night's sleep prefigures death, as we lie still, insensible. On the sickbed we cannot tell what day, what week, or what month we will rise—if ever. Being bedridden fetters my feet and manacles my hands as surely as if I were chained in stocks. I can feel my sinews and ligaments going slack.

In the grave I will continue to speak: through the epitaph on my gravestone, in the memories of my friends, in the words I leave behind. Here on the sickbed, I am my own ghost. When I try to converse with visitors, I frighten them. They conceive the worst of me, and yet fear even worse. They give me up for dead now, and yet wonder how I am when they awaken at midnight; tomorrow they will ask how I am faring.

It's a miserable, inhuman posture, though common to all of us. I must practice for death by lying still, but cannot practice my resurrection by rising anymore.

REFLECTION

MY GOD AND MY JESUS, my strength and salvation, you rebuked your disciples for scolding those who brought children to you. *Let the little children come to me,* you said (Matthew 19:13). Is there a truer child than I am now? Your servant Jeremiah protested, *I do not know how to speak; I am too young* (Jeremiah 1:7). O Lord, I am a sucking child and cannot eat, a crawling child and cannot move. I have a childish temper: I can't sit up and yet I hate to go to bed.

Lord, how can I approach you from this bed, hardly our normal meeting place? Are you accusing me, punishing me for former sins by stretching me out on this bed? Isn't that like hanging a man on his own door, to confine a sick man on his own bed of promiscuity?

David swore to you that he would not go up into his bed till he had built you a temple. When we *choose* to go to bed, that shows strength and our need for renewal. How can I come to you, though, when you have nailed me to my bed? You are still active in my congregation but I, their pastor, am locked in solitary confinement.

When the centurion's servant lay sick at home, his master rushed to Christ because the sick man couldn't. When their friend was paralyzed, four charitable men brought him to Christ. Peter's mother-in-law lay sick of a fever and Christ came to her, for she could not come to him. Friends in the congregation may likewise bring me before you in their prayers, and I must await your visitation, helplessly.

I lie imprisoned in bed, my slack sinews serving as iron fetters and these thin sheets as iron doors upon me. I lie here and say with the psalmist, *Lord, I love the house where you live* (Psalm 26:8). Yet I cannot go to your house, the church. I am not turning away from you; rather, I am prevented from worship. I feel excommunicated, and I yearn for fellowship.

You love action, Lord, and I am a preacher impaired from fulfilling my calling. In the grave no one can praise you and in the door of the grave, this sick bed, no one can hear me praise you. You touched my lips so that my mouth would extol you before others. Now the fear that gripped Paul is tormenting me, that *when I have preached to others, I myself should be a castaway* (1 Corinthians 9:27). Downcast, I'm afraid that I too may be cast away.

There is another station—or should I say prostration—even lower than this sick bed. Tomorrow I may be laid upon the floor and the next day lower still, into the grave, the womb of the earth. Now God suspends me between heaven and earth, like a meteor. An earthly body restrains me from heaven and a heavenly soul sustains me on earth.

You could carry me away in a chariot, as you did Elijah. Instead, you've chosen your own private way to carry me home, the same means by which you carried your Son. First he lay upon the ground and prayed. Then he had his exaltation (the word he used for his crucifixion). Only after descending into hell did he ascend.

Your hand has struck me into this bed, Lord Jesus. Therefore, if I do happen to recover, I trust you to redeem the rest of my life, by making the memory of this sickness beneficial to me. And if my body falls even lower, you will take my soul out of this sweat bath and present it to your Father, washed again, and again, and again, in your own tears, in your own sweat, in your own blood.

PRAYER

O MOST MIGHTY AND MERCIFUL GOD, though you have knocked me off my feet, you have not separated me from my foundation, which is yourself. Though you have felled me from an upright posture, in which I could stand and see the heavens, you have not dimmed that light by which I can see you. Though you have weakened my knees so that they cannot bow to you, the knees of my heart are bowed to you forever.

You have made this bed your altar; now make me your sacrifice, as you made your Son Christ Jesus. He is the priest, so make me his deacon, to minister to him by cheerfully surrendering my body and soul to your pleasure, by his hands. I come to you, O God, by embracing your coming to me. I come in the confidence that David showed when he said, *The Lord sustains them on their sickbed and restores them from their bed of illness* (Psalm 41:3).

Sustain me on this bed, Lord, so that whichever way I turn, I will turn to you. I want to feel your hand on my body, and on my bed, so that I will accept both correction and refreshment as flowing from one and the same source, your hand.

You have made the feathers of this bed thorns, in the sharpness of this sickness. So, Lord, make these thorns feathers again, feathers of your dove, the Holy Spirit. With me in this vulnerable position, Lord, do not say to me, "Now I am meeting you in the same bedroom where you so often departed from me."

Having burned up this bed by fiery fevers and washed It in abundant sweats, O Lord, re-make my bed and enable me to *commune with mine own heart upon your bed, and be still* (Psalm 4:4). Provide another bed for my former sins while I lie on this bed, and a grave for my sins before I come to my grave. And when I have deposited those sins in the wounds of your Son, allow me to rest in the assurance that my conscience is washed clean and my soul is free of danger.

Do this, O Lord, for his sake, your Son our Savior, Christ Jesus, who did so much in order that you might, in your justice as well as in your mercy, do so for me.

6

CALLING THE DOCTOR

THE HUMAN BODY, with its multitude of parts, is a little world. If those parts were stretched out across the globe—the veins in our bodies extended to rivers, the sinews extended to the veins of mines, the rippling muscles to hills, the bones to quarries of stones, and all the other parts stretched out in proportion—the sky itself could not contain us.

In this expanded world of the body, our thoughts are like invisible giants that travel from east to west and from earth to heaven, traversing not only all the sea and land, but reaching out to the stars, comprehending them all. Inexplicable mystery: despite being confined in the prison of my sickbed, I can send thoughts to the sun and beyond.

More, as the outer world produces serpents and vipers, worms and caterpillars—malignant, venomous creatures who devour the very world that gives them birth—so this world of ourselves produces venomous and infectious diseases that feed on and consume us. O miserable abundance, O counterfeit riches! Not only do we lack remedies for every disease, for many of them we have no name.

But we do have a Hercules to do battle against these monsters: the physician, who musters all the forces of nature to relieve the patient. We must call on doctors, for we require their expertise and training. Indeed, we don't even possess the healing instincts of animals. I've heard that a deer, pursued and wounded by an arrow, knows an herb which brings healing to the wound. Even the hunting dog, when sick, knows to eat the grass that restores its health.

Without the innate instinct for natural medicines, we frail humans must summon the pharmacist and physician. I take back all my musings on the exalted human being: how can I speak of our expansive greatness when disease so easily reduces us to a handful of dust. What has become of my soaring thoughts when sickness brings me to the blankness, the thoughtlessness, of the grave?

I lie helpless and alone, at home; it's time to send for the doctor.

REFLECTION

I MAY NOT HAVE THE RIGHTEOUSNESS of Job, but I have the same longing: *I desire to speak to the Almighty and to argue my case with God* (Job 13:3). My God, how soon should I call on the physician, and how far should I trust him? I know you have made the medicine, and the doctor, and the art of healing, and I'm not forsaking you when I turn to the physician. You didn't make clothes until the first humans felt shame about the naked body, but you did make remedies before there was any sickness, for you provided natural medicines from the beginning.

Did you create the remedies with the intent that we

would soon need them? No more than you intended that we sin when you created us. You foresaw both consequences, but caused neither. You desire for us health, not sickness. "Do you want to get well?" your Son asked when he encountered someone with an affliction. Every time, he responded with healing.

Is it a danger, though, for me to entrust myself wholly to the physician, to rely on him to such an extent that I neglect the spiritual healing that I also need? Reveal to me your plan, O Lord, and guide me in a way that gives you glory and me pardon. I pray your servant David's prayer, *Have mercy on me, Lord, for I am faint; heal me, Lord, for my bones are in agony* (Psalm 6:2).

I know that my weakness may appeal to your mercy, and my sickness offers an occasion for you to send me health. Respond to my misery with compassion, I pray. By your grace, I've used this time to repent of sin, and to give to others a portion of the little that you have given me. I've done my part, and now I'm ready to send for the physician.

I must say, though, that I hope to hear from my doctor the words that Peter said to the man bedridden for eight years: *Jesus Christ heals you. Get up and roll up your mat* (Acts 9:34). I long for the power of the Lord to heal me.

PRAYER

O GOD OF HEALTH AND STRENGTH, take a look at me. Beset by the fury of two diseases, I need two physicians, one for the body and one for the soul. I bless and glorify your name that, in both cases, you supply the help I need. You are life, and our health descends from you.

Heal me, O Lord, for I want to be healed. Keep me away from those who falsely profess the art of healing the soul or the body, by means not given by you in the church or in nature. No spiritual health can be had by superstition, nor bodily health by magic. You are the Lord of both kinds of healing, and in your Son you are the physician. *With his stripes we are healed*, prophesied Isaiah (53:5); even before Jesus was scourged, we were healed with his stripes.

You have promised to heal the earth, if its inhabitants would only pray. Heal this earth, O God, by repentant tears, and heal these waters, these tears, from all bitterness, from all diffidence, from all dejection, by implanting in me an unshakable faith. Your Son *went about healing all manner of sickness* (Matthew 4:23). No disease incurable, none difficult—he healed them all in passing and left no relics of the disease. Will this universal physician pass by this hospital, and not visit me?

If this day must be my last, seal to me my spiritual health. Meanwhile, my bodily health is now in the hands of others who can aid me; may they do so in a way that most glorifies you, and most edifies those who observe their care.

7

QUARANTINE

IF OUR GREATEST MISERY IS SICKNESS, its greatest misery is solitude. Fear of contagion daunts the helpers I need, and even the physician hesitates to visit. As a result, I lie here alone, isolated, a torture that hell itself does not threaten.

When I'm dead, and my body might infect others, then a remedy exists: they'll bury me. Yet when I'm sick and might infect, they have no remedy but to stay away, abandoning me to my solitude. Contagion offers a ready excuse to supposed friends who pretend to care, but really don't. At the same time, it blocks those helpers who truly want to assist, because they would risk becoming carriers of infection to others.

A long sickness will weary the best of friends, but an epidemic wards them off from the outset. To patients like me, it seems a kind of prison sentence, separating us from both companionship and charity.

Solitude goes against the natural order, for all of God's actions manifest a love of community. Heaven itself contains ranks of angels and a communion of saints. Everywhere we look, plurality rules: in the species, in the stars and their planets, which might include other worlds like ours. On earth, families, cities, churches, and colleges all comprise multitudes. Immediately after pronouncing creation good, God saw that it was not good for humans to be alone. So he made Adam a helper, one to increase our number on earth.

In contrast, with an infectious disease I'm sentenced to solitude, left utterly alone. It feels even worse than a grave, because although I'm alone in both, only in my bed do I know it and feel it. And in my bed, though not in my grave, my soul remains trapped in an infectious body.

REFLECTION

O GOD, MY GOD, your Son did not object to Martha when he said to her, *Your brother Lazarus will rise again* and she expressed disappointment, *I know he will rise again in the resurrection at the last day*—for he knew her immediate grief and misery (John 11:23-24). Don't object, then, when I remind you that *Two are better than one* and *pity anyone who falls and has no one to help them up* (Ecclesiastes 4:9-10).

I know your Son often felt isolated and lonely. Yet at any time he could have commanded *more than twelve legions of angels* to his service (Matthew 26:53). As he said, *I am not alone. I stand with the Father, who sent me* (John 8:16). I don't doubt that I'll always be with you, but I have no idea whether this disease may estrange my friends and loved ones. I don't doubt that you view my deteriorating state with compassion, but what about the others, who watch my mind and spirit decaying—how will they respond?

I can't endure this agony alone. My spirit can't survive without you, for I have lost the support of family and friends.

If you abandon me, I am woefully alone. Elijah himself faltered under that prospect: *I am the only one left, and now they are trying to kill me too* (1 Kings 19:10). Neither could Jeremiah reach for a stronger lament than to say, *How deserted lies the city, once so full of people!* (Lamentations 1:1).

Israel banished those with leprosy to live alone. Have I such a leprosy in my soul that I must die alone, shunned by those who would comfort me, and alone without you, my God?

I must stop, for my complaints are verging on blasphemy. I remind myself that Moses was commanded to approach the Lord *alone*, and that God came to Jacob when he was *alone*, and then wrestled with him through the night (Genesis 32:24). Perhaps a state of solitude and desertion best disposes us for God's drawing near? Like Jacob, am I left alone to wrestle with you and with my conscience, Lord, in a manner that would not occur if others were there to console me?

But there is hope. The Lord has provided for me, in one person, a physician who is also my loyal friend.

PRAYER

O ETERNAL AND MOST GRACIOUS GOD, who only once called down fire from heaven upon sinful cities, and only once opened the earth to swallow blasphemers, you have shown your mercy often. At the very beginning, you gave Adam a helper fit for him. So, whether you wish to preserve me longer on this earth, or to dismiss me by death, I plead for the help I need to face either possibility.

I ask that you protect this body from infections that may prevent some from visiting, or endanger those who do come. Also, guard my soul from any disorder that might shake my assurance that you will love me through my end. Close the doors of my heart, my ears, my house, to any usurper who might seek to undermine my faith in my time of weakness, or to defame me after my death with false rumors that I died doubting you. May I stand as an example to others that you were my God, and I your servant, to the very end.

Bless the learning and work of this doctor whom you sent to assist me. Since you have taken me by the hand and put me into his hands, I entrust him with my hopes, and you with my prayers, without conditions. *Thy kingdom come, thy will be done*: prosper him and relieve me, in your way, in your time, and in your measure. Amen.

8

FEAR

I STUDY THE PHYSICIAN with the same diligence as he studies the disease. I notice that he's scared, which scares me all the more. As he deliberates, I overtake him, I outrun him in his fear. Obviously, he's trying to disguise his fear, which makes me even more anxious. Doctors know that a patient's fear will very likely hinder his efforts toward healing.

Just as damage to one organ can affect every vital sign in the body, so fear insinuates itself in every process of the mind. Likewise, as gas in the body can counterfeit any disease and seem like gout or gallstone, so fear will counterfeit any disease of the mind. What seems like love might be the suspicious fear of jealousy. What seems like courage in the face of danger might only be fear of losing face. A man who's not afraid of a lion may be frightened by a cat.

What is it that I fear right now? Not death so much, but rather the progression of the disease. I would belie nature if I denied that fear, and I would belie God if I dreaded death. My weakness comes from nature; my strength comes from God.

I tell myself that not every chill is a plague, nor every shivering a stupor; neither is every fear a panic, nor every wish for relief a protest or a sign of despair. My physician doesn't let fear impede his work. I must not let my own fear prevent me from receiving from him—or God—the assistance and consolation that I need.

REFLECTION

FEAR CAN SUFFOCATE A RELATIONSHIP. Before he had the courage to address you directly, your servant Job said of you,

> He is not a mere mortal like me that I might answer him,
>   that we might confront each other in court.
> If only there were someone to mediate between us,
>   someone to bring us together,
> someone to remove God's rod from me,
>   so that his terror would frighten me no more.
> Then I would speak up without fear of him,
>   but as it now stands with me, I cannot. (Job 9:32-35)

You command me both to speak to you and to fear you—don't those two cancel each other out? Yet there is no contradiction in you, my God, my sun and my moon, who directs me as well in the night of adversity as in my day of prosperity. I must then speak to you at all times. When, then, must I fear you? At all times too.

Have you ever reproached a beggar for being troublesome? You gave us the parable of a judge who relented at last because of the tenacity of a client, in order to make the point that we *should always pray and not give up* (Luke 18:1-8). In another, you told of a man in bed at midnight who rouses himself to a pounding on the door, not because of friendship but because of his friend's very audacity (Luke 11:5-8).

God is always available. Pray in your bed at midnight, and God will not say, I will listen to you tomorrow on your knees. Pray upon your knees, and God will not say, I will hear you at church on Sunday. Prayer is never out of season, for God never sleeps and is always present. But God, how can I freely converse with you, in all places at all hours, if I fear you? Dare I ask this question? There is more boldness in the question than in the answer. You welcome my approach though I fear you; I cannot make that approach except I fear you.

Indeed, you have arranged that if we fear you, we need not fear anything else. *The Lord is my help and my salvation, whom shall I fear?* (Psalm 27:1). Great enemies? No enemies are frightening to those who fear you. What about famine? *The lions may grow weak and hungry, but those who seek the Lord lack no good thing* (Psalm 34:10). Never? Though that may be true for a time, conditions could worsen. *Why should I fear when evil days come?* asked David (Psalm 49:5). Even though his own sin had made the days evil, he feared them not. What about when the evil results in death? We need not fear even the sentence of death if we fear God.

Quite the opposite, you make others to fear us: *Herod feared John and protected him, knowing him to be a righteous and holy man* (Mark 6:20). How fully then, O God, how gently do you ease from me any qualms about fearing you. This must be what you mean when you say, *The Lord confides in those who fear him*—thus imparting the secret of fear's right use (Psalm 25:14). Have fear and benefit by it; be directed by it, and not dejected with it.

Of course, not all fears are beneficial. There is a fear that weakens us for God's service. *You of little faith, why are you so afraid?* you once admonished your disciples (Matthew 8:26). There is also a fear that is a consequence of former sins. And those who reject you are a prey to all fears. Yet you would give us a proper fear as a kind of ballast to carry us steadily in all weather.

Paradoxically, fear and joy go together. The women who first heard from an angel about the resurrection ran from the tomb on legs of *fear and joy.* Love, too, coexists with fear. In many places we are called upon to fear God, and yet the underlying command is, *You shall love the Lord your God*; whoever does not both, does neither.

David and his son Solomon both affirmed that *The fear of the Lord is the beginning of wisdom* (Psalm 111:10, Proverbs 1:6). A wise person, therefore, is never without fear. Although I pretend to no other measure of wisdom, I am rich in this, abundantly. I lie here possessed of fear, both that this sickness is your immediate correction and not merely an accident, and that it is a fearful thing to fall into your hands. Nevertheless, this fear preserves me from all undue fears, because you will never let me fall out of your hand that upholds me.

PRAYER

O GOD OF ALL TRUE SORROW and true joy too, of all fear and all hope too, as you have given me a repentance not to be repented of, so give me a fear of which I may not be afraid. Give me tender and sensitive emotions, so that as I joy with those who joy and mourn with those who mourn, may I also fear with those who fear. Meanwhile, since I'm perceiving my own danger through the fear of the doctor who has come to assist me, let me not shirk the necessary task of preparing myself for the worst, the passage out of this life.

Although many of your blessed martyrs left this life without evidence of fear, your most blessed Son did not. The martyrs were human, and therefore it pleased you to fill them with your Spirit and power, to make them more than human. In contrast, your Son, declared by you to be God, was required to show himself as a man. Let me not be ashamed of my fears, O God, but let me feel them as he did, submitting all to your will.

After you have inflamed and then thawed my former coolness with this fever, and quenched my former heat with these sweats, and corrected my former negligence with these fears—after all that, O Lord, be pleased to think me fit for you. Whether it be your pleasure to dispose of this body, this garment, by putting it to a further wearing in this world, or to lay it up in the common wardrobe, the grave, for the next world, glorify yourself in your choice now, and glorify it then, with the glory your Son has purchased for those who will partake in his resurrection. Amen.

9

CONSULTATION

I SENSE MORE FEAR in my physician, and therefore more cause for fear in me. If the physician appeals for help, the disease must be thriving. An autumn is drawing near, though I don't know whether it's the disease's autumn or my own. If mine, we both will die, for the disease cannot outlive me.

As for my doctor, he has shrewdly called in others for consultation. If the danger is dire, he now has witnesses to help determine his choice of treatment. And if the danger is not so great, he is humbly sharing the credit and honor for the work that he began alone. Either path shows wise leadership.

It doesn't diminish a monarch when he relies on others' wisdom. The Romans began with one king, then experimented with two consuls, then in emergencies returned to one dictator. Regardless, the state is healthier when policies are carried out by group counsel rather than by one ruler. Diseases seem to conspire how they may cooperate to destroy a body—shouldn't we then expect physicians to consult together in order to oppose them?

We live on the knife-edge of mortal danger. Death looms at an old person's door, hinting at its presence, while it also sneaks up in ambush at a young person's back. Anything may kill us—a poison, choking on a feather, even an allergic reaction to our best medicines. Some have died of joy, such as the poet Dionysius, who succumbed to a drinking bout held to celebrate his award for a triumphant play.

To maintain our health, I say, the more assistants the better. I should view the specialists who crowd into my room not as harbingers of death, but as guardians of life, a chorus of comforters.

And yet, even as I trust myself to the custody of my physicians, I cannot help commiserating with those who lack such care. How many lie sicker than I, laid in their woeful straw at home, with no more prospect of help if they die, than of comfort if they live. They don't expect to see a doctor, and the first person that takes notice of them is the sexton who buries them in oblivion. The numbers of these poor souls fill the daily charts of the dead, but we will never hear their names until we read them in the book of life along with our own.

How many lie sicker than I, thrown into hospitals, where (as a fish left upon the sand must await the tide) they must await the physician's hour of visiting, and then get only a brief, casual visit? How many lie even sicker, and have no hospital to house them, nor straw to lie on and die on? Homeless on the street, they have their gravestone beneath them, and breathe out their souls before passersby who avert their gaze. They have no medicine, no nourishment: for them ordinary porridge would be sustenance, discarded leftovers a tonic, the scraps from our kitchen tables nutriments.

O my soul, when you are not grateful enough to bless God for his mercy in affording you many helpers, remember how many lack them, and do what you can to assist them.

REFLECTION

MY GOD, YOUR SERVANT AUGUSTINE begged of you that Moses himself might come and explain what he meant by some passages of Genesis. May I ask similar guidance from your Spirit who inspired your book.

I believe that when the apostle Paul wrote to Timothy, *Only Luke is with me,* he did so with a touch of complaint and sorrow (2 Timothy 4:11). Although Luke was an able and faithful partner in the apostle's work, yet Paul felt alone with only Luke present. Indeed, Luke was a physician, which suggests that we may need more than one physician by our side.

When Moses' father-in-law persuaded him to unburden himself of the details of government, O God, your own Spirit moved Moses to delegate the work among seventy elders of Israel, even though Moses had gifts superior to them all.

Or, I think of how you employ numbers of angels. *Let all God's angels worship him,* Hebrews says of your Son (1:6). When on earth, Jesus said *that he could command twelve legions of angels* (Matthew 26:53) and at the last day when heaven and earth shall be one, *the Son of man shall come in his glory, and all the holy angels with him* (Matthew 25:31).

A choir of angels announced Jesus' birth to the shepherds, and two announced his second birth, the resurrection, to Mary Magdalene. Jacob dreamed of a multitude of angels ascending and descending on a ladder, the portal between heaven and earth, between you and us. Angels hasten us away from places of danger and temptation, as they did Lot from Sodom (Genesis 19:15), and transport our souls after death, as they did the beggar Lazarus (Luke 16:22). We see the power of individual angels, for in one night a single angel destroyed almost two hundred thousand in Sennacherib's army (2 Kings 19:35), yet you often employ more than one to minister to your servants.

We have four writers of the gospels, not one. And before he ascended, Jesus himself appointed numerous others to carry on his work. I entrust my soul to the universal communion of your church and to the bread and body of your Son, that through all the merits of his death he might restore me in this world and establish me in the next. Your way, from the beginning, has been to multiply your helpers, and so it would be ungrateful for me not to accept the mercy of many helpers for my bodily health.

PRAYER

O ETERNAL AND MOST GRACIOUS GOD, you gave manna to the Israelites in the wilderness, a kind of bread so constituted that to every person it tasted like their favorite meal. I humbly beseech you to make this illness, which I accept as part of my daily bread, to taste so to me—not as I would but as you would have it taste. Your corrections may taste of humiliation and at the same time of consolation, may taste of danger and also of assurance.

As your fire dries, so it heats too; and as your water moistens, so it also cools. O Lord, may both these operations work on my soul: that affliction may turn me to you, and that when it shows me that I am nothing in myself, it may also show me that you are all things to me.

In my current condition, O Lord, the one you have sent

to assist me has had to appeal to others for assistance. I see in how few hours I can fall beyond human help. Let me by the same light see that no fury of sickness, no temptation of Satan, no guiltiness of sin, no bodily prison—not this sick bed nor the other prison, the close and dark grave—can remove me from the good purpose that you have determined for me.

Open my eyes to the meaning of this illness. When I have read it in the language of correction, allow me to translate it into another, and read it as a mercy. Your mercy or your correction: which of these is the original and primary message, and which the translation, I cannot conclude, though death may conclude me. For though it certainly feels like a correction, I can have no greater proof of your mercy than to die in you, and by that death to be united to him who died for me.

10

THE KING'S PHYSICIAN

IN THE DOMAIN OF HUMANITY, kings occupy the highest ground, the most eminent hills. Yet what misery can rival sickness, and kings are as vulnerable to it as their lowest subject. Physicians hover about them, and they live in constant fear of falling ill.

Are they gods, these kings? If so, sick gods. What kind of god needs a physician? The true God is called sometimes angry, and sorry, and weary, and heavy, but never sick, for then God might die, as our gods do. We sometimes scorn the gods of the pagans by saying that perhaps they were sleeping—but gods too sick to sleep sink even deeper.

Those we esteem express their likeness to God better in their humility than in their highness. When, like God, they overflow with goodness and share their abundance with the needy, then they are gods. Healthy people appreciate the great gift of wellness, and welcome it with cheerfulness and joy; more, they desire to share that happiness and joy with others. Therefore, it perfects the happiness of kings to confer honor and riches—and, as they can, health—upon those who need them.

The gracious king has sent me his own physician.

REFLECTION

I REMEMBER A WARNING from a wise man, that "when the rich speak everyone stops talking, and then they praise the discourse to the skies. The poor speak and people say, 'Who is this?' and if he stumbles, they trip him up yet more." Therefore, I hesitate to speak of kings.

King David incorporated himself in his people, calling them his relatives, his bones, his flesh. When plague fell upon them, he cried, *I have sinned; I, the shepherd, have done wrong. These are but sheep. What have they done? Let your hand fall on me and my family* (2 Samuel 24:17). I acknowledge that you, O God, who gave sage Augustus an empire, gave it to wicked Nero as well. Though some kings deface your image through their actions, still they reflect something of your image in their reign.

If I failed to celebrate your mercies bestowed by my own sovereign, I would add the fault of ingratitude to my many other failures. I pray for the happiness and prosperity of my king. But as soon as I do so, I stop and think how this will look to others. Will I simply be puffing myself up, bragging that I am receiving from him some preferential treatment? Let not that false humility stop me, O God, but let me go forward, extolling your mercy channeled through him. After all, what he has done in assisting my bodily health, he has done for many others. When he can't heal with his own hands, he sends the gift of his physician.

My king's concern for my health, you know, O God, is but the twilight of the day. Before anyone else, he saw potential that I might be of some use in your church, and hinted, persuaded, and nearly ordered me to embrace that calling. You, who put that desire into his heart, also put into mine an obedience to his call. At a time when I was sick with dizzy indecision, it was this man of God who set me straight.

When I asked for a stone, he gave me bread; when I asked for a scorpion, he gave me a fish—when I asked for a secular position, he did not refuse me but instead convinced me for the ministry. These things, O God, you who forget nothing have not forgotten, though possibly he has. Not only has he sent a physician for my bodily health, he has been the physician for my spiritual health.

PRAYER

O ETERNAL AND MOST GRACIOUS GOD, you have reserved your treasure of perfect joy and perfect glory to be given by your own hands. At that time we will see you as you are and know you as we are known, possessing in an instant and forever all that can contribute to our happiness. Meanwhile, here in this world you give us a down payment in advance, a token of the treasure that awaits us.

As we see you here in a darkened mirror, so we receive from you here gifts of grace in common things. Nature reaches out her hand and gives us corn, and wine, and oil, and milk; yet you filled her hand before, and opened it so that she may rain down showers upon us. Industriousness reaches out her hand and gives us the fruit of our labor; but your hand guides that hand when it sows and when it waters, and yours is the increase. Friends reach out their hands and strengthen us, but your hand supports the hand that supports us.

From all these instruments I have received your blessing, O God. I bless your name most for the greatest gift, that by your powerful right hand I have had a part not only in the hearing but in the preaching of your Gospel. Humbly I pray, that as you pour out your goodness on the world by these instruments—the same sun and moon, the same nature and industry—so continue blessing this nation and this church.

When your Son comes in the clouds, may he find the king, or his son, or his son's sons, ready to give an account and able to stand in judgment for their faithful stewardship and use of the talents so richly committed to them. Be to him, O God, in all distempers of his body, in all anxieties of spirit, in all holy sadnesses of soul, such a physician in your proportion, who art the greatest in heaven, as he has been to me in his proportion, who is the greatest upon earth.

11

DIAGNOSIS

ARRAIGNED IN THESE FETTERS, I have presented my evidence, as if dissecting my own anatomy for a court trial. Now the doctors deliberate on my fate.

Masters of the art of medicine can scarce name all the sicknesses. Some, such as pleurisy, they name from the place affected, the *pleura*. Others they name from the effect it brings about, such as "falling sickness" [epilepsy]. The varieties of sicknesses are so many, however, that they must also extort names from other languages, from animals, from who discovered it or what famous person suffered from it. Even so, the number of illnesses exceeds the number of names.

Experts have analyzed my fever, meticulously comparing it to a near-infinite variety of fevers, in order to determine which is mine, and what it will do to me, and how it may possibly be subverted. I suppose I should be grateful that at least they have time for deliberation.

In many diseases, the side effects are so violent that the physician must treat them while ignoring the underlying cause, the disease itself. I see the same pattern in government. Sometimes insolent leaders stir up protest and disorder among the people. Those in power declare martial law and suppress the people, when actually the protest is a mere symptom of the real problem: injustice and oppression. The same applies to diseases of the mind and passions. If an angry man is about to strike a violent blow, I must break the blow before dealing with the root cause of his anger.

In all these cases, time is a gift. Where there is room for consultation, things are not so desperate. My doctors carefully consult and come to agreement on a treatment, so that nothing is rashly done. After receiving my own report of the disease, they concur on the proper remedy. It doesn't really help for them to chide me on what I should have done before, such as change my diet or exercise. That would be like telling a prisoner on death row: you might have lived if you had done this or that.

I rejoice that my helpers have knowledge (I've hidden nothing from them), that they consult (they hide nothing from each other) and that they write out a plan of treatment (they hide nothing from the world). Mostly, I rejoice that they propose remedies for my condition.

REFLECTION

THE PROPHET ISAIAH ASKED, *Who can fathom the Spirit of the Lord, or instruct the Lord as his counselor?* (40:13). O God, though you need no counsel from human beings, yet you do nothing regarding us without consultation. From the very beginning you conferred—*Let us make mankind in our image* (Genesis 1:26)—for all your external acts are decided within the Trinity.

I remind myself that all the blessed persons of the Trinity are conferring now on what you will do with this infirm body, and this leprous soul. Guiltily, yet trustingly, I await your decision. I don't pretend to advise those specialists who are discussing my body, though I describe to them my every symptom, anatomizing my body for them. So I do with my soul to you, O God, in a humble confession.

There is no vein in me that is not full of the blood of your Son, whom I have crucified again and again, by multiplying my sins. There is no artery in me that has not the spirit of error, the spirit of lust, the spirit of folly; no bone in me that has not been nourished with the marrow of sin; no sinews or ligaments that do not tie sin and sin together. Yet, O blessed Trinity, if you are hearing this confession, then my case is not desperate, my destruction is not decreed.

Clearly, you intend my ultimate healing. I find comfort and hope in your first book, the book of life, always open before you; and in your second book, the book of nature, where you have placed your own image; and in the third book, the Scriptures. To these you have added the book of doctrine in the church, the book of our own consciences, and finally the scroll with seven seals which only *the Lamb who was slain was found worthy to open* (Revelation 5:5-6).

If you refer me to a new reading of these books, a new trial by them, this fever may prove as temporary as a burn on the hand. I may be saved: not by my own conscience or by the other books, but by your first, the book of life that records my election, and by the last, the book of the Lamb who shed his blood for me.

If my bodily health is still under consultation, I am not

condemned yet. And according to these books, I shall not be condemned at all. Though even a late repenter will grasp your promises with desperation, the one who seeks you early will receive your morning dew, your seasonable mercy, your calming consolation.

PRAYER

O ETERNAL AND MOST GRACIOUS GOD, you have such pure eyes that you cannot look upon sin, and we have such impure natures that we can present little besides sin. We might fear that you would turn your eyes from us forever. But though we cannot endure afflictions in ourselves, yet in you we can; in like manner, though you cannot endure sin in us, yet in your Son you can. He has taken upon himself, and presented to you, the very sins in us that might displease you.

Look upon me, O Lord, with your compassionate eye that heals by its very gaze. In my distress, recall me from the border of this bodily death. Raise me from spiritual death, for I have wandered even to the jaws of hell, by multiplying heaps of sin on the foundation of original sin. Include me again in your consultations, O glorious and blessed Trinity.

The Father knows that I have defaced the divine image received at my birth. The Son knows I have neglected my interest in redemption. O blessed Spirit, as you are to my conscience, so be to the other persons of the Trinity: a witness that at this minute I crave what I have so often rebelliously resisted, your promptings. Be my witness that, in more pores than this slack body sweats tears, this sad soul weeps blood.

I suffer more from displeasing my God than from the stripes of God's displeasure.

Take me then, O blessed Trinity, into a reconsultation, and prescribe my remedy. If my body must suffer a long and painful holding of my soul in sickness, that is medicine, if I can discern your hand behind it. And if I should face a speedy departing of this soul, that too is medicine, if I can trust your hand to receive me.

12

STEALTH SYMPTOMS

THIS IS NATURE'S NEST OF BOXES: the heavens contain the earth; the earth, cities; and cities, people. All are subject to decay and ruin, and in each of them, the most dangerous threats are the ones most difficult to detect. When the Israelites were wandering in the wilderness, God knew their many grievous sins, but charged them with one: the inward rebellion of murmuring. Secret sins are the most deadly and pernicious.

In states and kingdoms, the noise from twenty rebellious drums poses less danger than a few whisperers and furtive plotters. The cannon doesn't imperil a wall as much as a mine under the wall; nor a thousand boisterous enemies compared to a few conspirators who take a solemn oath of silence.

So, too, with diseases of the body. In my case, the urine, sweat, and pulse have all sworn to say nothing, and thus disguise the sickness inside. My strength is not enfeebled, and I've regained my appetite. My mind remains clear, unclouded by anxiety. And yet my doctors see invisibly, and I feel insensibly, that the disease is prevailing.

My illness has established an empire within me, and it will advance by certain arcane secrets of state, which it is not bound to declare. Against state secrets, judges have the power of subpoenas; and against mysterious diseases, physicians have their expert investigators. These, they now employ.

REFLECTION

SAINT AUGUSTINE WISHED that Adam had not sinned, in which case Christ need not have died. I sometimes wish that, if indeed the serpent once walked upright and spoke to Eve, then he would do so still, in which case I could detect his presence! Instead he creeps, and as a result, spiritual death climbs stealthily through our windows—into our eyes and ears, the inlets of the soul.

Sometimes we sin in secret, so others may not know. In order to keep those sins hidden, Satan tempts us toward that which was his offspring from the beginning: a lie. The sin itself is the serpent's, and the lie its covering garment. The serpent's true masterpiece, however, is to entice us to sin so subtly that we may not know we are sinning. Our consciences seared, we do not feel the sting of the serpent or his venom. David prayed, *But who can discern their own errors? Forgive my hidden faults* (Psalm 19:12).

Other sins we conceive in the dark, upon our bed, yet commit them in the light. In fact, many sins we wouldn't even commit if nobody knew about them. Augustine confessed that he was ashamed of his tender conscience, and committed sins for the sole reason of impressing his companions.

In the end, we can never conceal sins, for you, O God, know them. The voice of Abel's blood told you of Cain's murder. You need no informer, for *you will bring every deed into judgment, including every hidden thing* (Ecclesiastes 12:14); and *there is nothing concealed that will not be disclosed, or hidden that will not be made known* (Matthew 10:26).

However, I acknowledge a better way for you to know my sins, one that you prefer: to hear them by my confession. As medicine works by drawing the foreign invader to itself, so your Spirit brings my former sins to my memory that I may confess them. *When I kept silent,* says David, *day and night your hand was heavy on me*; but when I said, *"I will confess my transgressions to the Lord" you forgave the guilt of my sin* (Psalm 32:3-6).

So thoroughly do you cleanse that you arm us against relapses into the sins that we have confessed. Augustine says, "You have forgiven me those sins which I have done, and those sins which only by your grace I have not done." These are most truly secret sins, because they were never done. The very tendency to sin needs your mercy, and receives your pardon. No other person, nor I myself, but only you know how many and how great are the sins I have escaped by your grace.

PRAYER

O ETERNAL AND MOST GRACIOUS GOD, how shall I present to you those sins that are unknown to me? If I accuse myself of original sin, will you ask me if I know what original sin is? I don't know enough of that doctrine to satisfy others, but I know enough to condemn myself.

If I confess to you the sins of my youth, will you ask

me if I know what those sins were? I don't remember them well enough to name them all, nor am I likely to live long enough to name them (for I did them then faster than I can speak them now). But I know them well enough to know that nothing but your mercy is as infinite as they.

Sins of thought, word, and deed; sins of omission and action; sins against you, against my neighbor and myself; sins unrepented and sins relapsed into after repentance; sins of ignorance and sins against the warning of my conscience; sins against your commandments; sins against the laws of the church and the state—so many sins, I cannot possibly name them.

Pardon me, O Lord, for all those sins for which your Son Christ Jesus suffered—for he bore all the sins of the world. There is not one among them that would not have been my sin, if you had not been my God, granting me a pardon in advance through your preventing grace.

13

THE HEART

ALWAYS IN MOTION, PUMPING LIFE to all the rest, the heart is the seat of the body's vitality. Yet if an enemy dares to rise up against it, no part capitulates more quickly. The brain may withstand a siege, and the liver even better, but an over-stressed heart will succumb in a minute.

Although the heart lacks strength, we respect it as the eldest, the first organ to form in the developing child. From its throne the heart reigns over its subjects, preeminent despite its weakness, for on it the entire body direly depends. When treating an illness, a wise physician may overlook some other ailing member of the body and instead devote primary attention to the heart, without which all parts will perish.

As king of the body, the heart attracts the venom and poison of every pestilential disease, just as the king of a nation attracts the malignance of evil men. And as the very best medicines lose their effectiveness when overused in the body, so the best attributes of leadership eventually yield to personal attacks by an enemy.

How small and vulnerable is the heart, the source of a body's life, and yet susceptible to wounds and infections from both outside and within.

REFLECTION

MY GOD, YOU ASK OF ME only my heart: *My son, give me your heart* (Proverbs 23:26). Is that all it takes, to become adopted as your child? You once challenged Satan, *Have you considered my servant Job? There is no one on earth like him; he is blameless and upright, a man who fears God and shuns evil* (Job 1:8). Shall I offer the opposite challenge: Have you considered my heart, more perverse than any on earth? Would you have that heart, and shall I become your son, a coheir with your eternal Son, simply by giving it to you?

The heart is deceitful above all things and beyond cure. Who can understand it? The one who poses the question receives the answer: *I the Lord search the heart.* (Jeremiah 17:9-10). When did you search my heart, Lord? Did you imagine finding it as pure as the one you implanted in the first human, Adam? You've searched humans since and found that *every inclination of the thoughts of the human heart was only evil all the time* (Genesis 6:5).

Do you still want my heart? O God of all light, I know that you know all things, and you are the one who reveals what is in our hearts. Without you, I could not know how sick my heart is.

I look to your Word, and there I find that despite the flood of evil that washes over all hearts, you found a man, David, after your own heart. Through the prophet Jeremiah you promised *I will give you shepherds after my own heart, who will lead you with knowledge and understanding* (3:15). And as I study the book, I find willing hearts, learned hearts, wise hearts, straight hearts, and clean hearts. If my heart were like these, I would give it to you.

On the other hand, in the same book I also find stony hearts, hardened like mine. I find hearts that are snares, as mine has sometimes been, and hearts that burn like ovens with the fuel of lust and envy and ambition, which have also burned in mine. *Whoever trusts his own heart is a fool* (Proverbs 28:26). Hearts like these—including mine—are not worthy to be offered to you. What shall I do?

To those of the first kind, the good hearts, you give a joyfulness of heart, which I don't pretend to have. To those of the second kind you give a fearful heart, which thankfully I don't yet have. There must be a middle kind of heart, not perfect but mendable in the very act of surrender, and not so soiled as to be rejected. A melting heart, a troubled heart, a wounded heart, a broken heart, a contrite heart—these I have, thanks to the powerful working of your Spirit.

Samuel told Israel, *If you return to the Lord with all your hearts, prepare your hearts unto the Lord* (1 Samuel 7:3). If I prepare my heart, I trust you to carry it home. No, I must admit that the preparation is your work as well. This melting, this breaking, this contrition—these discomforts in my soul are the sign of the Spirit at work in my heart, and God will finish the work that has begun.

This illness presents a bitter pill, O Lord, which has made me reticent around you. Today you have given me another morning, though, and my heart beats on. My heart seized up when I numbered my sins, but that pain is not terminal, because those sins are not terminal. Rather, my heart lives in you.

As long as I remain in this great hospital, this sick and polluted world, and as long as I remain in this leprous body, the heart that you have prepared will be subject to malign invasion. But I have my medicine in your promise: that when I know the plague of my heart and turn to you, you will preserve that heart from the deadly force of its infection, and *the peace of God, which transcends all understanding, will guard my heart and mind through Christ Jesus* (Philippians 4:7).

PRAYER

O ETERNAL AND MOST GRACIOUS GOD, whereas your presence fills all the rooms equally in heaven, here on earth your presence may seem more evident in some places than others—more in the church than in my bedroom, more in the sacraments than in my prayers. If the same applies to the parts of my body, I humbly ask you to manifest your presence more in my heart than elsewhere.

Into the house of your anointed king, traitors will enter; into your house, the church, hypocrites will enter; into the house of my body, temptations and infections will enter. Make my heart your abode, O my God, and bar these intruders from any access.

Your Son himself had a sadness in his soul, an apprehension of death, but he had a remedy too: *not my will, but yours be done.* You have the power to make this present sickness my everlasting health, this weakness my everlasting strength, my very faintness of heart a powerful balm. When your blessed Son cried out, *My God, my God, why have you forsaken me?* you reached out your hand to him—not to deliver his sad soul, but to receive his holy soul.

I sense your hand upon me now, O Lord, and I don't ask why it comes and what it intends. Whether I stay in this body for some time, or meet you this day in paradise, I leave in your hands. My course of treatment is a silent and absolute obedience to your will, even before I know it. And when you have catechized me with affliction here, may I serve you in a higher place, in your everlasting kingdom of joy and glory. Amen.

14

BREATH

IF THE VERY AIR WE BREATHE might kill us, how can we ever be safe? To be killed by hailstones or by gunshot is one thing—but by breathing in air from another person? I realize I'm flirting with heresy by questioning God's design in nature, but shouldn't air nourish us, not destroy us?

If I suffered ill effects from breathing the vapors from a long-shut well, or a newly-opened mine, I would have nothing to complain about except bad luck. But when we ourselves are the well that exhales the poison, the oven that spits out the exhaust, the mine that spews out the droplets of death, then anyone—a neighbor, a friend, a relative, myself—may be a potential killer.

Oh, for something to blame! If I had any conscious part in my self-destruction, then I would chide myself. Excessive drinking or eating, intemperance, promiscuity—any of these may involve me in the murder plot. But what have I done? They tell me my melancholy may be a factor; did I invite melancholy into myself? Yes, I think too much; was I not made to think? I study excessively; doesn't my calling call for that? I've done nothing willfully or perversely, and yet I must suffer from it, die by it.

I know many examples of people who have been their own executioners. Some have kept poison close by, in a hollow ring on their finger, or in a writing pen. Some have beat their brains out on the wall of their prison, and one is said to have strangled himself despite having his hands bound, by crushing his throat between his knees. I, who have done nothing to harm myself, am somehow my own executioner.

I have heard of accidental deaths from the smallest things, such as the prick of a pin that leads to infection and gangrene. But to die from breathing in common air! What foul air that I may encounter in the street, or in a slaughterhouse, or a garbage heap or sewer, can do as much harm as what I have somehow inbreathed in my own home?

REFLECTION

MY GOD, YOUR SERVANT JAMES ASKS US, *What is your life?* and then provides the answer: *You are a mist that appears for a little while and then vanishes* (4:14). If he asked me, *What is your death?* I would give the same answer: *it is a mist too.* Why should it trouble me whether I live or die, if life and death are the same, both a mist?

You have made mist so neutral a substance that it can represent both your blessings and your judgments. In Eden *a mist came up from the earth and watered the whole surface of the ground* (Genesis 2:6). Later, priests offered sacrifices to you that went up in a fragrant cloud of incense. On the contrary, what is sin but a vapor, a smoke that takes away our sight and blinds us to danger? At the end of time, a prophet foretells, *When he opened the Abyss, smoke rose from it like the smoke from a gigantic furnace* (Revelation 9:2).

Have you supplied us no way to evaporate these smokes, to dissipate these vapors? You did just that, by descending to assume our nature, in your Son. And even though our last act will be an ascension to glory, our first act is to follow the way of the Son by descending. At the baptism of your Son, the Spirit descended, and at Pentecost the same Spirit descended. Let us draw out and purify the vapors of our own pride, our own wits, our own wills, our own inventions, by the cleansing power of your sacraments and by obedience to your Word.

PRAYER

O ETERNAL AND MOST GRACIOUS GOD, though you allow us to destroy ourselves, you have provided means of repair and healing. Subdue, I pray, any breath of disobedience to you so that I may, in the power and triumph of your Son, tread victoriously upon my grave.

You have laid me low in this valley of sickness, so low that I echo the question asked of the prophet in a field of bones, *Can these bones live?* (Ezekiel 37:3). So I ask you, in your good time, to carry me up to the mountain where you dwell, the holy hill, a place where no one can ascend save *the one who has clean hands and a pure heart* (Psalm 24:4)—which none can have but by that one strong way of making them clean, in the blood of your Son, Christ Jesus. Amen.

15

A RASH

WE SAY THE WORLD IS COMPOSED of sea and land, as though they were equal, but we know there is more sea in the Western than the Eastern hemisphere. We say the sky is full of stars, but we know that more are visible at the Northern than the Southern pole. We say life consists of misery and happiness, as though equally distributed, with as many good days as bad. The truth is far from that perfect balance.

Misery we drink, but happiness we merely taste; misery we harvest, and happiness we only glean; in misery we journey while in happiness we barely walk. Misery is undeniable, verifiable; happiness is elusive, hard to pin down. Everybody feels misery as misery, while happiness means different things to different people.

By its spots my sickness now declares itself to be a pestilential disease, like the plague. My symptoms should now make the diagnosis easier, though whatever comfort I find in that fact is overshadowed by fear that the disease may have advanced beyond the reach of treatment. Perhaps the physicians have already done all they can. It gives no consolation to identify an enemy, only to find that this enemy has an overwhelming force that guarantees its victory.

In wartime, voluntary confessions are more reliable than confessions extracted through torture. When nature itself cries out through symptoms on my body, I pay attention. But what if my body has induced this rash, perhaps as an allergic reaction to the medicines already tried? I could no more trust such symptoms than an interrogator could trust the forced confessions of a traitor.

We take scant comfort from knowing the worst when the worst is incurable. A woman welcomes the birth of her child with joy, her body relieved of a burden. Yet if she could see into the child's future—how irresponsible, how ungrateful toward her the child might prove to be—her mind may receive a greater burden.

So much of life mixes sorrow with joy, and so much happiness turns out to be spurious. Even what we think of as virtues are tied to misery. I must be poor and needy before I can exercise the virtue of gratitude, pushed to the limit before I can exercise the virtue of patience.

How deep we dig, and for such impure gold! And what other measure of happiness have we than comparison: how my happiness compares to that of others, or to my own at other times? I have little hope of regaining health when these spots only tell me I am worse off than I was before.

REFLECTION

MY GOD, YOU HAVE MADE this sick bed your altar, and I have no other sacrifice to offer but myself. Will you accept a spotted sacrifice? Does your Son, unblemished, so dwell in me that you see no spots? How can your Son not have spots when he took on himself all our stains and defects? And the church, your bride—every part of that fair body is marred with stains and spots.

Lord, if you seek spotlessness, where will you find it? Your mercy may go a long way in my soul and yet not leave me without spots; your corrections may go far and burn deep, and yet not leave me spotless. The rain you send upon us does not always soften our hard soil; you kindle fires in us that do not burn up all our dross; you heal our wounds and yet they leave scars.

The spots you hate are the ones we hide. No matter how my flaws reveal themselves—by natural course, by voluntary confession, or by your correction—regardless, you receive that revelation with grace. *It is not the healthy who need a doctor, but the sick*, said your Son (Matthew 9:12). Until we are forced to face the symptoms of our illness and confess our spots, you apply no medicine.

My sins, my defects are part of what your Son came down to earth to gather and assume to himself. When I present my spots, I present him with what is already his, and until I do so, I withhold what he came for. May I look upon these spots on my chest, and on my soul, not as the pinches of death, but rather as the constellations of the sky, to direct my contemplation to that place where your Son is, at your right hand.

PRAYER

O ETERNAL AND MOST GRACIOUS GOD, accept my humble thanks for this particular mercy, hard as it seems. Even in your corrections, I find comfort.

I know, O Lord, the anxiety that accompanies the phrase, "the house is visited," when a physician finds a dwelling whose inhabitants bear the marks of plague. Perhaps you leave your own marks upon a patient, but what a wretched hermitage is the house *not* visited by you, and what outcasts are those who have none of your marks upon them. These fevers, O Lord, which you have brought upon this body, are but the melting of the wax that will seal me to you. These spots are but the letters in which you have written your own name and conveyed yourself to me.

Whether you take me now, or in a later exchange by glorifying yourself in my stay here, I don't care. Only be present to me, O my God, and this bedchamber and your abode shall be all one room, and the closing of my bodily eyes here, and the opening of the eyes of my soul there, all one act.

16

CRITICAL DAYS

I DON'T MEAN TO PORTRAY the human condition any worse or more miserable than it is—as if that's even possible. Think about it. As material beings, we're hemmed in by time. Our happiest days are soon overtaken by our most miserable days. Time flows like a swift river, swallowing everything in its path, and no one can stop or control it.

We say that time divides into three parts: past, present, and future. But the past has already disappeared, the future doesn't yet exist, and the present is so fleeting that as soon as you say the word it has joined the past. In such a flimsy, half-nothing interval we experience a few stray moments of happiness.

And if you consider time in relation to eternity, our history on earth appears as a tiny parenthesis in a volume that has no end. From that perspective, the most durable earth creature lives but a minute, and human life is a mere second compared to that of a tree, or the sun. Of that sliver of eternity, how much offers an opportunity for satisfaction or pleasure?

What people strive after—honors, awards, possessions— lose their luster over time. Today's celebrities will be forgotten by the next generation. As they advance in age, the highest achievers will lose the capacity even to remember their accomplishments, and will leave all their possessions behind. Youth is the time for ambition, when honors and pleasures mean something. For the aged, they come too late, like medicine arriving after the church bell has already announced death, or a pardon granted after the beheading has taken place.

We rejoice in the warmth of a winter fire, but does anyone huddle before one at midsummer? Or are the pleasures of spring appropriate in autumn? If happiness depends on the season, or the climate, how much happier are birds, who can fly away to enjoy the same climate year-round. Trapped in time, we humans have no such luxury.

REFLECTION

MY GOD, MY GOD, would you call yourself the Ancient of Days if we were not someday to be held accountable for our days (Daniel 7:22)? Would you chide us in the parable for *standing here all day long doing nothing* if we knew we'd have plenty of time to bring in our harvest (Matthew 20:6)? When you instructed us to *not worry about tomorrow, for tomorrow will worry about itself,* should we take that literally (Matthew 6:34)?

Days matter. Paul tells us, *now is the time of God's favor, now is the day of salvation* (2 Corinthians 6:2), and, elsewhere, *put on the whole armor of God, that you may be able to stand in the evil day* (Ephesians 6:11). How we spend our days gives a strong clue to our spiritual health, for if the soul withers the healthiest looking body is but an illusion.

Each of us has a critical day in confronting your Son. The

Pharisees sought to pin him down over the issue of paying taxes to Caesar; the Sadducees tried to entrap him with a question about the resurrection; and an expert in the law tested him with a question about the greatest commandment. Jesus handled them all: *No one could say a word in reply, and from that day on no one dared to ask him any more questions* (Matthew 22:15-46).

I sense I am entering my critical day with you, even as my body is entering a critical state. In such a crisis, a skeptic may look to forsake you, to shake off the shackles of religion and strike out with a spirit of freedom. But, God, I claim the holy boldness of Jacob who, though you lamed him, would not let go until you had given him a blessing (Genesis 32:26). Though you've laid me upon my hearse, I won't let go until you've seen me through this crisis, which holds my life in the balance.

Since *a day is like a thousand years* with you (2 Peter 3:8), I ask that my critical "day" stretch out for a week. On the first day, I ask you to join me in my place of sickness, for your presence counts more than anything else. The second day, I devote to the light of my conscience. I'll begin in the evening, reviewing the sad guiltiness of my soul, and await the cheerful rising of your Sun. I'll begin dejected and accused, and end that day purified and acquitted by your Son.

On the third day, I'll prepare myself by receiving your Son in the sacrament of communion. Though the eucharist has been entangled in many unnecessary debates, I take it as spiritual nourishment: just as bread and wine is assimilated into my body, so is the body and blood of your Son imparted to me in the same action.

After walking with you for three days, I'll be ready for the storms of my fourth day, the day of my demise. This somber day, I'll mark by fasting, in preparation for my death. At last, that event will deliver me over to my fifth day, the day of my resurrection. And this day of awakening will present me, reapparelled in my own body, with body and soul united, to my sixth day, the day of judgment. That day is the most critical of all, for it will lead to my seventh day, my everlasting Sabbath of rest.

From then on, I won't need to number my days anymore. I will live forever, in the presence of your glory, your joy, the sight of yourself.

PRAYER

O ETERNAL AND MOST GRACIOUS GOD, your light illumines not only the day, but the night as well. Though you have allowed some dimness, some clouds of sadness to darken my soul, I humbly bless your holy name, and thank you for the light of your Spirit, against whom the prince of darkness cannot prevail.

Except there were some light, there could be no shadow. Let your merciful providence so govern this sickness, that I never fall into utter darkness, or ignorance of you, or thoughtlessness. Overcome the shadows of my faint spirit, O God of consolation. Overwhelm my bouts of self-condemnation by the power of your irresistible light. When such clouds gather overhead, may your Spirit disperse them, and establish me in a bright day, a crucial day, one in which I may accept your judgment. Give me confidence in what your Son promised: *Behold I am with you always, even to the end of the world* (Matthew 28:20).

17

INSOMNIA

SLEEP HAS A DOUBLE BENEFIT: it renews the body in this life and prepares the soul for the next. In the very act of rejuvenating us, sleep prefigures death. We lie down in hope that we'll rise renewed, while at the same time we lie down aware that we may never rise again. Sleep is an opiate that gives us blissful rest, though with the risk that we might not awaken from its spell.

God originally intended sleep for our bodily rest alone, not to prefigure death. After the fatal choice in Eden, however, God mercifully tempered our fear of death by giving us the tamer, more agreeable form of sleep. Now I awake from a nightmare and realize my vivid fears were unfounded; perhaps death will be like that too, a sudden rousing into a new and peaceful reality. As we need sleep to live out our span on earth, so we need death to enter an eternity that we can't outlive.

Here is my torment: while my sickness keeps the enemy death constantly before me, insomnia robs me of the refreshing sleep that I need to keep death at bay. Even prisoners on death row get to sleep at night until their fateful time comes. If I'm about to enter eternity, where there is no distinction of hours, why must I keep staring at the clock, longing for sleep?

Oh, if only the heaviness of my heart would affect my eyelids too. Since I've already lost delight in all worldly objects, why can't I close my eyes in sleep to shut them out? And why can't I get a moment's sleep to prepare me for a state of continual waking?

REFLECTION

MY GOD, I KNOW YOU HAVE SAID, *he who watches over Israel will neither slumber nor sleep* (Psalm 121:4). But what about those you love, the ones over whom you are watching? *You grant sleep to those you love*, you once promised (Psalm 127:2). Will you now take away from me the very evidence of your love? *You will lie down and no one will make you afraid*, you once pledged (Leviticus 26:6); am I now deprived of that protection?

Jonah slept during one horrific storm and your Son slept through another one. I can't even sleep in my own bed on a calm night. Your disciples said of their friend Lazarus, *Lord, if he sleeps, he will get better* (John 11:12). Where does that leave me, who can't sleep at all?

I console myself that I'm not the only one who suffers from insomnia. Some mischief-makers *cannot rest until they do evil; they are robbed of sleep till they make someone stumble* (Proverbs 4:16). The rich lose sleep worrying about their investments. Besides, sleep has its own pitfalls. When Samson fell asleep on Delilah's lap, it led to his downfall (Judges 16). The guards at the tomb of your Son concocted the lie that they were sleeping when his body was stolen away, and some believed them. Since Jesus rebuked his disciples for sleeping at Gethsemane, shall I complain because I can't sleep?

In the Bible, sleep is often used as a euphemism for death, and sometimes as a sign of sin. *So then, let us not be like others, who are asleep, but let us be awake and sober*, admonished your apostle (1 Thessalonians 5:6). I must therefore look more closely into the act of sleeping before I misinterpret my sleeplessness. Your hand upon me is light, O Lord; shall I blame any finger of that hand for being too heavy?

As a pastor, I am called to be a watchman, a seer, with eyes wide open. Though my body feels sick and weary, yet my soul lies in peaceful rest with you. As my eyes can look beyond the earth, up unto the stars, so may my eyes see past my present circumstance and instead fix themselves upon your peace, and joy, and glory above.

Almost as soon as the apostle wrote, *let us be awake and sober*, he added, that Christ *died for us so that, whether we are awake or asleep, we may live together with him* (1 Thessalonians 5:10). Although my absence of sleep may hint of the presence of death, yet this gentle sleep and rest of my soul betroths me to you, to whom I will be bound indissolubly, by means of my dissolution.

PRAYER

O ETERNAL AND MOST GRACIOUS GOD, you are able to make the sick beds of your servants a chapel of ease, and the dreams of your servants a sanctuary of prayers and meditations upon you. Let not this insomnia that you have laid upon me be a source of disquiet or discomfort, but rather a sign that you don't want me to sleep in your presence.

Whatever this sleeplessness indicates about the state of my body, I'll leave in the hands of the physicians. I turn to you as the Physician of my soul. Remind me that I will ever wake toward you and yet will ever rest in you. Defend my soul, I pray, against all anxieties and distractions, especially those that would tempt me to think of any part of my sickness as a sin.

I brought sin into the world with me, and have since heaped upon it an innumerable multitude of sins. I have sinned behind your back (if that's possible), by willfully abstaining from church and from my service there. I have sinned before your face, by my hypocrisies in prayer, by my ostentation and pride in preaching your Word. I have sinned when my spirits are low, by complaining, and even when things go well, by being negligent of my faults.

Thankfully, my gracious God, I know that despite all those sins, you will consider me as I was when you first wrote my name in the book of life. So, no matter how I stray and wander in the midst of this illness, O God, I ask you to return to the minute when you were pleased with me, and accept me as you did then.

18

THE FUNERAL BELL

AN ITALIAN AUTHOR WROTE a treatise on bells while being held prisoner in Turkey. He would have plenty to write about if he were my fellow-prisoner in this sick bed, so near to the steeple that never ceases ringing out the sounds of death.

When the Turks conquered Constantinople, they melted church bells into armaments. I've heard the sounds of bells and armaments both, and none have affected me so much as these bells now. I have toured a steeple in Belgium which contains more than thirty bells, and one in France with a clapper said to weigh more than six hundred pounds, but neither impressed me as much as these outside my window. Here, I know almost every person whose funeral the bells announce. We lived as neighbors in houses close together, and soon I will be following them into their new abode.

Sometimes, I'm told, royalty or dignitaries correct their children vicariously, by punishing a surrogate child in their place, as a shaming lesson. When these bells announce that now one and now another is buried, I can't help feeling that they received the punishment due me, and paid the debt that I owe.

I've heard the story of a bell in Italy which rang

spontaneously when any member of the monastery was sick unto death. Once it rang when no one was sick, but the next day one of the monks fell from the steeple and died, preserving the bell's prophetic reputation. If these bells are merely warning of a funeral, perhaps my death is the one they're prophesying.

How many witnesses of an execution, if they would ask, "Why was that prisoner condemned?" could not substitute their own faults as an answer? I might have been that man being carried to his grave right now. I have the same mortality as the weakest among us, and was born to as many infirmities as they. Though some have preceded me in death, and at a greater age, I'm right behind them, advancing in record time with a vehement fever.

Yesterday I might well have been judged the more likely victim than whomever these bells call to the grave today. God holds the power of death in his own hands, lest anyone should bribe death. If we knew the gain of death, the ease of death, we might try to assist it, speed it along. Just as the ambitious watch others achieve and hope that success will fall upon themselves someday, so when these hourly bells toll another funeral, it gives me wry hope that the end of my misery may soon come.

REFLECTION

MY GOD, I HAVE A BONE TO PICK: not with you, but with those who object to the ceremony of bells at funerals. Some oppose the tradition because pagans practiced it—well, they conducted funerals too. Others object because Christians believe bells may drive away evil spirits. What of it? I don't doubt that the evil spirit is annoyed by the sound, for it serves to bring the congregation together and unite God and the people of God.

In the Old Testament, you sanctioned first the calling of the assembly by the sound of a trumpet, and then their gathering by the sound of the bells worn by the priests. Now the order is reversed: at death we enter the communion of saints accompanied by the sound of bells, and someday our bodily resurrection will take place with the sound of trumpets. Secular authorities use trumpets too, but bells are reserved for the sacred.

The man whose death these bells announce lay at home yesterday, at journey's end. His soul has moved on today, but the bells recall to us his acts and example, which will live on in our memories. Lying in bed, I could hear the congregation singing, and I joined in. I could not, however, hear the sermon, so these bells became like a sermon to me.

With this fever, O my God, do I need any more *memento mori*, reminders of my mortality? Perhaps as material beings we need these tokens, these devotional aids to our meditation. But isn't my voice, my own parched and hollow voice, reminder enough? Need I look upon a skull, when I have one in my shrunken face? Or contemplate death in my neighbor's house when I harbor death in my own breast?

PRAYER

O ETERNAL AND MOST GRACIOUS GOD, you have consecrated our living bodies to your own Spirit, making us temples of the Holy Ghost. Temples deserve respect, even when the priest has exited them, or when the soul has departed the body. I bless your name, for as you take care of every hair of our heads during life, we trust you with every grain of ashes after our death.

As you look after us in life and also in death, so you want us to do likewise to one another. I hear this brother, who is now carried out to his burial, speaking to me and preaching my funeral sermon in the voice of these bells. He speaks to me aloud from that steeple, and whispers to me in my bed: *Blessed are the dead who die in the Lord from now on* (Revelation 14:13).

Let this prayer, O God, be my last gasp, my expiring, my dying in you. If this is the hour of my departure, may I die the death of a sinner, drowned in my sins, saved in the blood of your Son. And if I live longer, may I die the death of the righteous, by dying to sin, which is a resurrection to new life. You bring death and give life. Whatever comes, comes from you; no matter what comes, let me come to you.

19

THE "PASSING" BELL

AH, NOW I HEAR A DIFFERENT RINGING of the bell; not a funeral bell, but one announcing a grave sickness just before a person crosses the threshold of life's end. Perhaps the poor soul is so sick as to not know for whom it tolls. Or—sudden thought—perhaps the attendants who see my decline have caused it to toll for me!

Regardless, I am joined to the same body, the church, and what happens to one member happens to all. When the church baptizes a child, that action involves me, for the child is ingrafted into the body of which I am a member. And when she buries a person, that action pertains to me as well.

All humankind has the same author, and populates the same volume. When one person dies, a chapter is not torn out of the book, but rather translated into a better language. God employs various translators—age, sickness, war, justice—and God's own hand guides every translation. That same hand will bind up all our scattered pages for an eternal library in which every book will lie open for inspection.

Therefore, as the bell that summons to a church service calls not just the preacher, but the entire congregation, so this passing bell calls us all. And especially me, brought so near the door by this sickness.

Recently a dispute occurred over which of the religious orders should ring the morning bell first to announce morning prayers, and it was decided that the one who rose first should ring first. If we truly grasped the gravity of this passing bell, we would rise early to contemplate its meaning, for all of us will die, not just the one who lies at death's door. The bell tolls for whoever thinks it does, and gives us an occasion to prepare for the time when we will be united to God.

Who doesn't look up to the sun when it rises, or to a comet when it streaks across the sky? Who doesn't incline his ear to a bell, wondering what prompted it? This bell that I hear signifies a passing of a piece of myself from this world. No one is an island, isolated and self-contained. If a chunk of earth be washed away by the sea, Europe is diminished—as much as if it were a promontory, or a friend's manor, or my own. Anyone's death diminishes me, because I am involved in all humanity.

Therefore, never ask for whom the bell tolls; it tolls for you, and for me.

It may seem as though I am absorbing misery from my neighbors with these morbid thoughts—as if I didn't have misery enough on my own. But in fact, affliction is a kind of treasure, for affliction can mature and ripen us, making us fit for God. If I carry my treasure as a lump of gold, not currency, it won't help defray my expenses as I travel. Similarly, tribulation is a kind of treasure, not very useful until the time we get nearer and nearer our home in heaven.

A neighbor is lying sick unto death, and this affliction may lie in his bowels like gold in a mine, of no apparent use to him. But the very bell that informs me of his affliction digs out and applies that gold to me. By considering his plight, I contemplate my own, and thus secure myself, by turning for help to my God, who is our only security.

REFLECTION

MY GOD, MY GOD, is this one of your ways of drawing light out of darkness, to make the one for whom this bell tolls, now in his dimness, to become an overseer, a bishop to as many as hear the message in the bell? Is this one of your ways, to raise strength out of weakness, to bring one who cannot rise from his bed to pay me a visit, and through this sound to give me some vital instruction?

O God, if you set your voice to it, what thunder is not a well-tuned cymbal, what strident tone is not a clear organ? And what organ is not well played if your hand be upon it? I detect your voice, your hand, in this sound, and in this one resonant note I hear the entire concert.

I hear Jacob assemble his sons before his death and say, *Gather around so I can tell you what will happen to you in days to come* (Genesis 49:1). I hear Moses telling me, as well as all who heard him, *This is the blessing I pronounce on you before my death*, so that we would consider our own death in his. (Deuteronomy 33:1). I hear your prophet saying to Hezekiah, *Put your house in order, because you are going to die; you will not recover* (2 Kings 20:1). I hear your apostle Paul saying, *I think it is right to refresh your memory as long as I live in the tent of this body, because I know that I will soon put it aside* (2 Peter 1:13-14).

In this passing bell, I hear a legacy, a last testament,

and now apply another's condition to my own benefit. Most importantly, I hear a voice that makes all sound music, and all music perfect: I hear your Son himself saying, *Do not let your hearts be troubled*, and *I am going to prepare a place for you* (John 14:1-2).

Permit me to ask one thing, though, my God: Since heaven promises glory and joy, why don't we experience more glorious and joyful things to induce us to heaven? In the Old Testament, you guaranteed your people wine and oil, milk and honey, abundance and victory, peaceful hearts and cheerful countenances—all to prepare them for the joys and glories of heaven. Why have you changed your way, so as to lead us by discipline and mortification, by mourning and lamentation, by miserable ends and miserable anticipations of these miseries?

Do we need a foil of depression and disgrace to contrast with the perfection of heaven, a sourness of this life to give us a taste for something better? I know, my God, it is far, far otherwise. But why, then, won't you let us have more joys and glories in this life?

Pardon, O God, my ungrateful rashness. Even as I ask the question, I find in my life reasons for gratitude. And if we do not find joys in our sorrows, and glory in our dejections in this world, we may risk missing both in the next.

PRAYER

O ETERNAL AND MOST GRACIOUS GOD, you have spoken to us in many ways: first in the voice of nature, which speaks to our hearts, and then in your Word, which speaks to our ears. Yet you have also spoken in the speech of speechless creatures, such as Balaam's ass (Numbers 22:28); and in the speech of unbelievers, such as in Pilate's confession (Matthew 27:24); and even in the devil himself, who recognized and addressed your Son (Luke 4:3). I humbly attend to your voice in the sound of this sad passing bell.

First, I thank you that in this sound I can hear your instruction, that I should use another man's condition to consider my own. Frankly, this bell that tolls for another's approaching death may take me in too, even before it finishes ringing. As the wages of sin, death is due me; as the end of sickness, it belongs to me. Though in view of my disobedience I may fear death, in view of your mercy I need not be afraid. Therefore I surrender my soul to you, which I know you will accept, whether I live or die.

Into your hands I commit my spirit, said David, placing himself under your protection (Psalm 31:5), and your blessed Son echoed those words when he delivered up his soul on the cross. Now I too surrender myself into your hands, submitting to your will, for life or for death, in your own time. I am prepared by your correction, mellowed by your discipline, and conformed to your will by your Spirit.

Having received your pardon for my soul, and asking no reprieve for my body, I boldly shift my prayers toward the one whose bell has inspired this devotion. Lay hold upon his soul, O God, and in however few minutes it remains in his body, let the power of your Spirit perfect his account before he passes away. Present his sins to him in such a way that he may not doubt your forgiveness but instead dwell upon your infinite mercy. Let him discern his faults, yes, but wrap himself up in the merits of your Son Christ Jesus. Breathe inward comforts to his heart, and afford him the strength to give an outward testimony, so that all about him may derive comfort from it, seeing that even though his body is going the way of all flesh, yet his soul is going the way of all saints.

When your Son cried out upon the cross, *My God, my God, why have you forsaken me?* he spoke not only for himself but for the church and its afflicted members who in deep distress might fear your forsaking. This patient, O most blessed God, is one of them. On his behalf, and in his name, hear your Son crying to you, *My God, my God, why have you forsaken me?* and don't forsake him. With your left hand lay his body in the grave (if that be your will), and with your right hand receive his soul into your kingdom. And unite him and us in one communion of saints. Amen.

20

THE DEATH KNELL

THE TOLLING OF THE CHURCH BELL has changed, from a faint and intermittent pulse to a strong and clear knell that marks my neighbor's transition to a better life. His soul has departed and—like a person who signs a thousand-year lease after the expiration of a short one, or who receives an inheritance after a life of debt—he has now gained possession of a better estate.

Where has his soul gone, though? Who saw it come in, or who saw it leave? Nobody. Yet everyone is sure he had a soul, and now has none.

If I inquire among philosophers, I'll find some who will tell me the soul doesn't exist; rather, the natural elements of the body somehow produce those faculties we ascribe to the soul. Nothing in us outlives the body, they say. They see nothing like a soul in other creatures, and reduce us to the level of beasts. But if my soul were no more than the soul of an animal, I could not be thinking such thoughts and reflecting on myself, something animals cannot do.

If I ask theologians how the soul, as a separate substance, joins the human body, I'll get mixed answers. Some will tell me that it generates from the parents. Others conjecture that it enters the body as a direct infusion from God.

If I ask church authorities what happens to the souls of the righteous as they depart the body, again I'll hear different answers. Some say they endure a period of purification, or purgatory, in a place of torment. Others suggest they'll enter the presence of God immediately; still others propose an interlude of rest before souls arrive at their final state.

St. Augustine studied the nature of the soul as much as anything (except the soul's salvation), and once sent an express messenger to St. Jerome to consult his wisdom. He satisfies himself with this: "Let the departure of my soul to salvation be evident to my faith, and I care the less how dark the entrance of my soul into my body be to my reason."

At this time, I'm more concerned with the soul's going out than its coming in. The bell tells me that a neighbor's soul has departed, but to where? I don't even know the man's identity, much less his spiritual condition and how he spent his life. I wasn't present at his sickness or his death, and from this bedside I can hardly quiz those who knew him.

I have only my charity, which tells me that he has gone to everlasting rest, and joy, and glory. I owe him that mercy, because I received the benefit of his instruction when the bell tolled, which motivated me to pray for him. I did pray, with faith, and so I faithfully believe that his soul has gone to everlasting rest.

But then there's his body left behind—what a wretched thing is that! The body that housed an immortal soul within minutes became a house that the soul couldn't flee fast enough. The body is a house no longer, because nothing dwells in it, and it's soon dissolving to putrefaction.

Who wouldn't recoil from seeing a clear and sweet river in the morning be polluted by muddy sewer-water by noon? That's a lame representation of what happens to the human body. All the parts that once worked together so harmoniously now deteriorate like a statue of clay with its limbs melting off, or like snow melting, or sand crumbling, so that nothing is left but dust, rubbish, and a pile of bone. This man whom the bell has declared gone—if he was a tailor, who comes to him now for clothing? Or for counsel, if he was a lawyer, or for justice if he was a judge?

The earth is our stepmother. After we grew in the womb of our natural mother, she delivered us to be planted and to grow to maturity in some place in the world. But in the womb of the earth we rot away, growing smaller, until finally our grave is opened to make room for another. We are not transplanted, but transported, our dust blown away with common dirt, with every wind.

REFLECTION

SOMETHING IS BOTHERING ME, LORD. Why, at your instruction, did Moses forbid priests to have contact with the dead, even to assist at their funerals (Leviticus 21:1-4)? What lay behind that puzzling ceremonial law?

I content myself with the answer that during those times the Gentiles showed excessive reverence for the memory of the dead. With over-zealous devotion they celebrated those who died, and preserved their memories with statues and likenesses and elaborate tombs. Over time, monuments became a source of idolatry, and people began worshiping and praying to lifeless images. *Why consult the dead on behalf of the living?* admonished the prophet Isaiah (8:19). Perhaps for that reason you instituted this strict law, lest the Israelites be tempted by the same practice of exalting the dead.

However, since we no longer face those dangers, surely we should treat the dead with reverence and learn from them. Meditating on the death of my brother should produce a better life in me. Indeed, it would be a kind of second death if I passed away with no one learning from the manner of my death. The death of others should catechize us to death.

Your Son Christ Jesus is called *the firstborn from the dead* (Revelation 1:5). He, the eldest brother, rises first, and is my master in the science of death. Yet the man whose death knell I heard also preceded me, as did everyone I know who has gone before me, and all serve as tutors to me in this school of death. From this neighbor who died I take away the same message as you sent to the church at Sardis: *You have a reputation of being alive, but you are dead. Wake up! Strengthen what remains and is about to die, for I have found your deeds unfinished in the sight of God* (Revelation 3:1-2).

Here is my strength: that whether you say to me as your angel said to Gideon, *Peace! Do not be afraid. You are not going to die* (Judges 6:23) or whether you say as you said about Aaron, *he will die there* (Numbers 20:26), yet you will preserve my soul from the worst death, that of willful rejection of your Spirit. I dare not resist your Spirit by ignoring the help you are offering me through my neighbor's death—I, whom the Lord of life loved so much as to die for me.

PRAYER

O ETERNAL AND MOST GRACIOUS GOD, I have a new reason for gratitude and a new reason for prayer, thanks to the ringing of this bell. The previous bell reminded me that I am mortal and approaching to death. In this one you may be telling me that I am in an irrecoverable, terminal state. If that's your message, I am indebted to you for speaking to me so plainly. Your voice is not the voice of a judge pronouncing a sentence, but of a physician prescribing a course of health. You present death as the cure of my disease, not its triumph.

If I've mistaken you and jumped to a conclusion by imagining death too near, even then I hear your truth. From the very first development after my conception, I've been moldering away. My whole life is an active death. Whether this voice instructs me that I am dying now, or reminds me that I've been dead all this while, I humbly thank you for speaking to my soul.

I pray for the time when our souls may be united to our resurrected bodies, for your Son Christ Jesus' sake. May that time come soon when your blessed Son will enter into his final office, that of a judge. Then sin, which you hate, will be cast into the grave, abolishing all of its instruments; the allurements of this world, and the world itself; sin's temporary revenges, the stings of sickness and of death; and all the castles and prisons and monuments of sin.

Time will be swallowed up in eternity, and hope swallowed in consummation, and ends swallowed in infinity, and all those ordained to salvation will be one everlasting sacrifice to you, where you may receive delight from them, and they glory from you, for evermore. Amen.

21

HOPE

ALL THIS TIME THE PHYSICIANS have been patient with their patient, scouting my body in search of any land in this troubled sea, any sign of hope. Each slight disorder of mine accelerates the rages of the disease, while nothing they do seems to speed recovery. We simply have to wait it out until the sickness ripens on its own.

A disease runs by its own rules—discordant, irregular, rebellious, beyond our control. In contrast, nature proceeds in an orderly and predictable way. We can't coax out July in January, or delay spring flowers until autumn. We can't command the fruits to come in May, nor the leaves to hang on through December. A pregnant woman can't postpone her delivery from the ninth to the tenth month for the sake of convenience; neither can a queen speed it up to the seventh month. Orderly nature won't allow such exceptions.

People in power don't like deviations either. Some of them are benevolent, and will do justice, but on their terms, in their own time. If you don't know their quirks, you may starve before receiving charity, or die before receiving pardon. One kind of tree won't bear fruit unless much manure be spread about it; similarly, some in power require much tending, cajoling, and bootlicking. Another tree requires pruning and lopping; some power brokers must be intimidated and threatened before agreeing to justice.

People have different personalities, and different vulnerabilities. Some respond to awards and honors whereas others care more about the approval of their friends and family. To succeed, we must learn to read those traits and know their seasons. How then can we succeed against a disease, which progresses in its own mysterious ways? All this time we've been fighting a defensive war, at a huge disadvantage. The enemy knows our weaknesses and we don't know his strength, and have no clue where he may next attack.

O, how many are besieged with this sickness, including many far more worthy and yet more miserable than I. They lack the sentinels of health, physicians, as well as munition from the pharmacists. They may well perish before any sign of reprieve in the illness. In my case, however, the siege has slackened giving us a ray of hope. At least I'll die fighting in the field now, and not helpless in prison.

REFLECTION

MY GOD, YOU ARE DIRECT and even literal, desiring to be understood according to plain sense. Yet at the same time you also speak in figurative, metaphorical language. Your words travel far and wide to capture rare images and allegories, and reach heights of expression that make all others seem like scribblings.

Just as you give us the same earth to labor on and to lie

in, you give us the same Word for comfort and reproof, for our instruction and our pleasure. Who but you could provide a book that convinces one person it's the Word of God because of its reverent simplicity, and another because of its majesty; one wonders why some readers can't understand it, and the other marvels that anyone can. Even your esteemed servants Jerome and Augustine, when puzzled, would consult unlearned old women and young maids to help discern the meaning.

As I think about it, you're a figurative and metaphorical God in your actions as well as your words. All through the Bible, the act of worship is a continual allegory, with types and figures flowing into other symbols and being transformed into still other figures. For example, circumcision prefigures the practice of baptism, and baptism points to the purity that we'll enjoy in a state of perfection in the new Jerusalem.

You spoke and worked in this manner through your prophets and also your Son. How often did Jesus use metaphorical language, calling himself a way, a light, a gate, a vine, or bread? This encouraged the early Christians to use the same style as they explained Scripture and composed both public liturgies and private prayers. Right now, their frequent use of the metaphor of water stands out to me.

My physicians have just given me hope, comparing my improvement to the discovery of land after a long and tempestuous voyage. The Bible also likens our calamities to the deep and turbulent waters of the sea. In the midst of a storm, it seems you will surely drown—and yet the very next day you might awaken to find the waters calm. And those who live on the Mediterranean think of it as a great sea because they've never seen the ocean. Similarly, we think our own afflictions the heaviest because we don't know what others are going through.

I've been through deep waters, O God, dealing with a sickness beyond my strength to resist. At such a time, I call on you for strength. As the psalmist says, *God is our refuge and strength, an ever-present help in trouble. Therefore we will not fear, though the earth give way and the mountains fall into the heart of the sea* (Psalm 46:1-2). Elsewhere it says, that you *gather the waters of the sea into jars and put the deep into storehouses* (Psalm 33:7). Your corrections are not wasted: when the waters have accomplished their task in humbling your patient, you shall recall them back to that storehouse.

I'm still unwell, riding out the waves, but at least you have provided an ark for me in the form of my physician. You could save us by a miracle, but usually you provide more natural means. St. Paul warned the centurion on his ship about a coming storm, but the Roman ignored the warning and ended up battling a Mediterranean hurricane for fourteen days. *Unless these men stay with the ship, you cannot be saved*, Paul told him, and this time he listened (Acts 27:31). May I trust the ship you have lent me for this storm, my physician, as well as your Son who knows how to calm the sea.

Forgive me for asking though, my God: If I have a sturdy ship, and faith in your Son the master of the seas, why aren't we nearer land? When the disciples took Jesus into a boat, *immediately the boat reached the shore where they were heading* (John 6:21). You can accomplish what you want whenever you want. Why the delay that dampens my hope?

I need the patience of your prophet, who said, *The Lord is good to those whose hope is in him, to the one who seeks him; it is good to wait quietly for the salvation of the Lord* (Lamentations 3:25-26). You put off many judgments until the last day; can't I endure the delay of your mercy for another day?

PRAYER

O ETERNAL AND MOST GRACIOUS GOD, you passed over infinite millions of generations before you created the world, and yet after you began that endeavor, you never ceased your work until you had perfected it and rested on the Sabbath. I have long exercised patience, waiting for some sign from you about this sickness. Now the doctors have hope. If my recovery will bring glory to you, I ask you to proceed and perfect that work.

Priests approached you in the temple by walking up steps, and angels came down to Jacob by descending a ladder. You, however, need no stairs; you can do anything, anywhere, all at once. Lord, I'm not weary of your pace, or of my own patience. I'm not asking for a different timetable, or some other outcome than the one you choose for me. It doesn't matter to me whether you do the work of a thousand years in one day or stretch out a day's work for a thousand years. With my recent improvement, I'm already tasting of the joy that awaits me in heaven someday.

These signs of improvement have come from you, and if I begin to explain them away as a natural occurrence, my hope will vanish because I'll not be trusting in you. If you should remove your hand completely from me, nature could easily destroy me; if you withdraw your healing hand, the powers of nature would prove impotent on their own. Therefore, let this day's good news be the promise of tomorrow's, as long as it aligns me with your will.

22

PURGING

THERE'S A TIME FOR TALK and a time for action. Discussion and debate don't always lead to a resolution, but we can judge actions by their effects. The best-conceived laws only prove themselves when a judge on the bench executes them; the councils of war are concluded when an army marches forth to carry out the agreed strategy.

In ancient times, diplomats were sometimes memorialized by a marble bust of their likeness, armless, with head and shoulders only on the block. Counselors of the state, they had contributed advice and policies, but were not the ones to carry them out. As the statue implied, they served as the head, not the hands. The same pattern applies to the arts and sciences. Creativity and imagination may begin in the head, but they find their full expression in something the hand fashions.

For days now I've heard the ideas and received the counsel of physicians. Their assistance has sustained me this far, and now they tell me that unpleasant action is needed. They wish to purge and starve my entire digestive system. The very notion seems a violation of nature: to empty that which provides nourishment, to weaken that which gives me strength. Do I not appear wasted enough already that now they need to subtract even more?

As if I needed more proof of human misery, now I learn that the very treatment designed to make me well first makes me sicker. It must be done now, they say. They'll slim me down, purge everything foreign from my body and, who knows, perhaps in the process annihilate me. O my over-cunning, over-watchful, over-diligent misery!

REFLECTION

MY GOD, YOU ARE A GOD OF ORDER, but not of ambition and competition. When will you put an end to the contentious quarrels over which has priority, faith or works? A healthy human body requires both the head and the hand; a functioning government requires both counsel and action; and a truly spiritual person needs to demonstrate both faith and works. So often you refer us to the kind of proof demonstrated by action: faith without works is dead.

Frankly, I'm a bit suspicious of tedious discussions and debates, which may allow the time for action to slip away. *Whoever watches the wind will not plant; whoever looks at the clouds will not reap* (Ecclesiastes 11:4). Fishermen must, of course, spend time mending their nets, but it may be sheer laziness if they sit around doing that instead of fishing. *Lazy hands make for poverty, but diligent hands bring wealth* (Proverbs 10:4).

I know, Lord, that you look upon our hearts, yet you also look carefully upon the work of our hands. *Who may ascend the mountain of the Lord? Who may stand in his holy place? The one who has clean hands and a pure heart* (Psalm 24:3-4).

In fact, sometimes the actions of head and heart are almost interchangeable. Often the Bible says *The Lord said* or *The Lord commanded*, and those very instructions were carried out by the hand of Moses or by the hand of the prophets.

Believing may precede it and suffering may follow, but *action* stands in the most obvious and conspicuous place in the life of faith. Why then, O God, have I been so slow to act? It took this illness for me to attend to my spiritual state, and shall I go no further? No, I must use this occasion to return to you as my center. Just as my body is cleansed by purging, I want my soul to be cleansed by confession.

The medicine used for purging the body is violent and contrary to nature, and the same applies to medicine for the soul. I'll submit myself to confession not out of a tortured conscience, but because I believe it to be good for me. *I will lift up the cup of salvation and call on the name of the Lord*, said the psalmist, after a close escape from death (Psalm 116:13). I will lift my cup, as full of contrition as it once was full of worldly frivolity.

Before his execution, your blessed Son was offered a cup to dull the pain, and refused it, instead embracing the whole torment. I will not drink such a cup either, but will first contemplate the cup containing my sins and then pour them out according to the guidance of your Holy Spirit and the ordinances of your holy church.

PRAYER

O ETERNAL AND MOST GRACIOUS GOD, I ask you, who joined this soul and this body in me, to heal me spiritually in the same way you are restoring me physically.

The physicians are now preparing to flush away the impurities that endanger my body. Lord God, I have a river in my body, but a sea in my soul, one swollen to the depth of a deluge. You have raised up hills in me by which I might have stood safe from these inundations. Education, observation, the examples of others can supply such hills; your church, your Word, and your sacraments rise even higher; the spirit of remorse, contrition, and repentance for former sin are hills too. I've rested on each of these peaks, but the deluge has surged even above them.

I have sinned and sinned, and multiplied sin to sin, even after all these defenses against sin, and where is there water enough to wash away this deluge?

There is a red sea, greater than this ocean, and there is an inlet through which this ocean may pour itself into that red sea. Let the spirit of true repentance and sorrow convey all my sins into the wounds of your Son, and I shall be clean. My soul will be much better purged than my body—fittingly, as it is ordained for a better and longer life.

23

RESURRECTION

IF THE FIRST MAN HAD BEEN LEFT ALONE in the world, would he have fallen? Even with no woman present, wouldn't Adam have been his own tempter? Knowing how weak we are now, and how easily we fall into sin even without a foreign tempter, should I think Adam any different? God saw that man needed a helper for him to be well; but to make woman ill, the devil needed no third party.

O what a giant we face when we fight against ourselves, and how diminished we are when we rely on our own strength. How small and how impotent is any one person alone. I can't rise out of my bed without my physician's help. When we're at the end of our rope, and death would come as a relief, even then we can't help ourselves. A prisoner being pressed to death might find it a relief to add a few more weights to finish himself off, but he can't even manage that additional misery.

I'm told I may rise, and I do so. But am I any better off? I feel more prone to collapse now that I'm up than when I lay prone in the bed. O perversity, even rising is a way to ruin!

Nature abhors a vacuum, as does human society. If a person gets promoted and fails to fill the new position, somebody else will soon take their place. Even the most virtuous leader may be undermined by false rumors of incompetency or corruption. No one who rises is safe from falling.

When I stand up, I grow light-headed and the world swirls about me. I'm an argument for what the astronomers now tell us, that the earth is spinning around and orbiting even though it seems to stand still. Humanity orbits one fixed point in life: misery. We try to take a step or two, and soon we're right back in the bed, miserable again.

For a long time I wasn't able to rise. Now I must be raised by others. Yet once I'm up, I am ready to sink lower than before.

REFLECTION

MY GOD, MY GOD, how like a mirror of the next world is this one! I get a glimpse of the resurrection of my soul in heaven by its likeness to my resurrection from sin on earth, as well as the rising of my body from this illness. I urge you to complete this resurrection, which you've begun, by bringing me back to health.

Correct me, O God, if I'm making an improper request, or asking for something that might turn out even worse. I have a bed of sin, in which I once delighted. More, I have a grave of sin, about which I once felt numb. Whereas Lazarus lay four days in a tomb, I've been putrefying for fifty years. Why don't you call me, as you did him, *with a loud voice*, since my soul is as dead as his body was?

I need your thunder, Lord; your music will not suffice. If

you want to be heard, you can make yourself heard—you've spoken to your prophets with sounds like those of a whirlwind, a chariot, a waterfall. When your Son and Spirit concurred with you at creation, you spoke in whispers, the members of the Trinity easily hearing one another. But when your Son came to earth and began the work of redemption, you spoke so loud that bystanders mistook the sound for thunder (John 12:28-29). John the Baptist announced the beginning of your Son's ministry with a voice like a town crier's; then Jesus himself announced its end with loud cries from the cross.

You proclaimed the Ten Commandments, Moses said, *in a loud voice to your whole assembly* (Deuteronomy 5:22). Without doubt you have a powerful voice that commands attention like no other. *The Lord thundered from heaven; the voice of the Most High resounded*, sang David after a great victory (2 Samuel 22:14). You speak with a voice mighty in volume, and also mighty in effect. An entire psalm celebrates the majestic qualities of that supreme voice (Psalm 29).

A time will come, said your Son, *when the dead will hear the voice of the Son of God and those who hear will live* (John 5:25). For me, Lord, that time is now. Why, then, can't I hear your voice? You speak loudest when you speak to the heart, and I want to hear a voice so loud that it drowns out all others. My sins cry out, as do my afflictions. I yearn for your responding voice to call me out of this bed and hold me upright.

I fear, O God, that my sinful memory will replay my old sins again, and instead of guilt I'll feel delight. I have survived this bed of death, even though I deserved that end, and indeed you have refreshed me while I lay here. When will you complete the work, bidding me to *take up my bed and walk* (Matthew 9:6)? My emotions lie in bed with me—when will I be able to control them again? My afflictions lie there too—when will I be able to bear them without lament? When shall I take up my bed and walk?

You are God over all flesh and all spirit. In my fainting spirit, content me with the gradual recovery that lies ahead for this decayed flesh. First I will learn to sit still, and then stand, and then walk, and by walking to travel. I pray that my soul, obeying this voice of resurrection, may likewise grow in grace step by step. May I become so surefooted as to remove all suspicions or jealousies between you and me, and may I speak and hear in such a voice that still I may be acceptable to you, and satisfied by you.

PRAYER

O ETERNAL AND MOST GRACIOUS GOD, you have made little things to symbolize great ones, such as the water of baptism and the bread and wine of your table. Receive my humble thanks that, not only have you granted me the ability to rise out of this bed of discomfort, but you have also given me a foretaste of a second resurrection, from sin; and of a third, to everlasting glory.

Though infinite, your Son was pleased to grow in the Virgin's womb and to grow in stature stage by stage. I know you have good purposes for me in your holy will; reveal them to me by degrees, in such a way that I find you to be better and better every day.

You allowed Saint Paul a "thorn in the flesh," a messenger of Satan to teach him that *your grace is sufficient* and your *strength made perfect in weakness* (2 Corinthians 12:7-9). I live by your grace. No matter what you furnish me today, tomorrow I'll perish if I don't have more. I have eaten of the bread of sorrow for many days, and now have tasted of the bread of hope. Continue, O Lord, feeding me the sustaining bread of life.

When you created angels, and then they watched as you produced fowl and fish and other animals, I'm sure they didn't badger you and say, Will we have no better companions than these? They waited, and then had humans delivered over to them, a species not much inferior to themselves. Similarly, now that I'm able to rise, I'm not complaining about the lack of immediate healing. I am practicing patience, learning in the school of affliction.

I have learned that my bodily strength is subject to every puff of wind, and my spiritual strength to every blast of vanity. Keep me therefore both grateful and humble: that I may have something to thank you for, which I have received, and something still to pray for and ask of you.

24

THE SOURCE

WHAT A RUINOUS FARM we take on in caring for the human body! On any day the dilapidated house may collapse, and diseases grow in the body like weeds overspreading the ground. As weeds cover not only every patch of turf but every stone too, so disease infects not only every muscle but every bone. Indeed, each tiny tooth is subject to a pain that can strike fear in the human heart.

We pay rent to our bodily landlord, in the form of meals twice a day, and spend half our time laboring to afford the rent. (The other half, we spend in sleep.) In addition, we pour medicines into that fickle body, then unwittingly expose it to more contagion by inviting family members and friends to contribute their own diseases!

Even though we tend our body like a farm, we cannot enjoy its bounty. No sooner do we pull out a weed of disease by the root than another, more violent one springs up. We treat it, and recover soundly, only to find the whole ground contaminated, the soil itself ruined. The body has a propensity to disease that requires constant intervention. We must study the soil that produces such ailments, finding it at times arid, at other times swampy, at all times barren.

The poor farmer works tirelessly to correct the soil, draining a swamp, importing soil and sand from elsewhere; and sometimes, like a phoenix rising from ashes, that barren soil bears fruit. But in my body I have taken on a more difficult farm. No part of my body, if amputated, would cure another part. And I can't accept help from another person, as in a transplant, without damaging the generous donor.

When I took on the task of managing this farm, my body, I found not a swamp to drain but a moat filled with water. I undertook to perfume dung, to extract rot and poison that had spread through every part. To cure the acute symptoms of disease is a great work, and to cure the disease itself even greater. But to cure the root, the source of disease, is a work reserved for the great physician, who can do so only by transforming these bodies in the next world.

REFLECTION

MY GOD, MY GOD, how can I identify, much less eradicate, the root, the fuel, the ultimate source of my sickness? What Hippocrates, what Galen, what expert physician could locate that in my body? It lies deeper, for it lies in my soul.

Since Adam's fall, sin is the source of all sickness and it permeates both body and soul. How can I prevent it, or how expel it? You might as well ask me to separate yeast from a lump of dough, or salt from the sea.

The whole world is a pile of kindling and embers on which we are laid, and do you expect us never to catch fire? No, we are the bellows that fuel the fire. Sometimes we do so in

ignorance, but in the Old Testament even sins done in ignorance required a sacrifice (Numbers 15:24). How much worse
are sins with knowledge: *Although they know God's righteous
decree, they not only continue to do these very things but also
approve of those who practice them* (Romans 1:32).

Human nature itself fans the coal and, paradoxically,
even the law does. St. Paul had not known what coveting
was until the law said, *You shall not covet*; then *sin, seizing
the opportunity afforded by the commandment, produced in me
every kind of coveting* (Romans 7:7-8). Perversely, we do some
things simply because it is forbidden. As Paul put it, *For in my
inner being I delight in God's law; but I see another law at work
in me, waging war against the law of my mind and making me
a prisoner of the law of sin at work within me. What a wretched
man I am!* (Romans 7:22-24).

Infinite temptations surround us, and as if that were not
enough, we're tempted by our own lusts. More, there are
times when we sin for the sake of others! Adam sinned for
Eve's sake; Solomon sinned to gratify his wives; Pilate and
Herod sinned to please the crowd. How manifold are the
ways to fall into sin.

Do you require me, O God, to purge myself of myself
before I can be well? When you bid me to *put off my old
self* and be made new (Ephesians 4:22), does that mean not
only my old habits of actual sin but the innate tincture of sin
imprinted by nature? How can I do that without falsifying
what you have also said, that sin infects everything?

Pondering the state of my body, I discern something of my
soul. No anatomist dissecting a body can say decisively "Here
lies the coal, the fuel, the source of all bodily diseases"; yet we

know enough about our own constitution and health that we can prevent many dangers. Similarly, though we cannot precisely locate the source of sin or eliminate it, yet through the water of baptism we have cleansed it. Sin may not disappear, but is weakened, and loses its former force. And though it may have the same name, it has been defanged.

PRAYER

O ETERNAL AND MOST GRACIOUS GOD, you are the God of security and the enemy of security both. In other words, you would have us always sure of your love, and yet always doing something in response to it. Give me the confidence of your presence with me, though I must not rely unduly on that confidence.

You granted Hezekiah an extra fifteen years of life, and renewed Lazarus's lease on life. Nevertheless, in both cases you gave only a reprieve, not a cure, to their mortality. You do the same with our souls, O God. You pardon sin, but do not immunize us against future sins; you make us acceptable, though not impeccable.

It would be impudent and ungrateful of me to look back on my sins, which in true repentance I have buried in the wounds of your Son, as if they could spring to life again and condemn me to death. They are dead in him who is the fountain of life. At the same time, it would be insolent and presumptuous to think that your present mercy would absolve all my future sins, or that there were no embers, no coals, of future sins left in me.

Temper your mercy to my soul, O my God. May I not grow faint in spirit, suspecting your forgiveness to be less hearty, less sincere than you have promised it to be. Nor may I presume that your mercy is an antidote against all poisons, and so expose myself to temptations with false assurance. I dare not cast myself into new sins, dare not exploit the mercy that you have already shown me.

25

RELAPSE

WHEN THE NIGHT BELL HAS RUNG in the city, you bank the fire, rake up the embers, and lie down to sleep in peace. Not so with the body. Long after you have raked up the embers of disease with medicine and diet, the fear of relapse persists.

We are most affected by pleasures we've personally tasted and enjoyed, and most tyrannized by pains that summon up memories of our own past afflictions. A patient passing a kidney stone wonders how anyone can call the gout a pain, while someone who has felt neither condition may fear a toothache just as much. Only compassion allows us to feel the pangs of another's suffering.

When we have ourselves experienced a torment, however, we tremble at the threat of relapse. We have panted through all those fiery heats, sailed through all those overflowing sweats, watched through all those sleepless nights, and mourned through all those long days. We have stood before the bench waiting for the physicians to finish consulting and deliver the verdict. We know precisely what lies ahead, and that knowledge fills us with dread.

Often, we bear some responsibility for the relapse because of something we have done or not done, which only adds to the suffering. Not only do we stand under a falling house, but pull it down upon us; not only are we executed, but are our own executioners.

When first we fall ill, we take some comfort in the fact that everyone is vulnerable to disease. With a relapse comes guilt and self-accusation: "How irresponsible I am, how ungrateful to God and to my helpers, in destroying so soon their good work in delivering me from my illness." The affliction leaps from my body to my mind, which ruminates on the sinful carelessness that must have led to my relapse.

To make matters worse, a recurrence attacks more swiftly and violently, more irremediably, because it finds the host weakened and decimated. A new sickness we can scarcely fear because we don't know what to fear. But with a relapse, we know exactly what to fear, and fall helpless before it.

REFLECTION

MY GOD, MY GOD—mighty Father who has been my physician, glorious Son who has been my medicine, blessed Spirit who has applied all to me—shall I alone overthrow the work of all three, and relapse into those spiritual sicknesses from which your infinite mercies have healed me?

I have received more than my portion of your mercy, yet my measure was nowhere near as large as that of your numerous people, the glorious nation of Israel, and how often they fell into relapses! How, then, can I feel secure? You overlooked many other sins in them, but vehemently reacted against those into which they so often relapsed: murmuring against you and your servants, and embracing the idolatries of their neighbors.

O my God, murmuring is a slippery slope to an irrecoverable bottom, whether it's directed against you or to the ones who represent you. You work through chosen leaders. They are the garments in which you clothe yourself, and whoever shoots at the clothes cannot say he meant no harm to the one wearing them. Oftentimes, murmuring that begins against a leader ends up with the people turning away from you. For Israel, today's murmuring became tomorrow's idolatry, and they frequently relapsed into both.

The soul of sin is disobedience, no matter what form it takes. When one sin dies, it transmigrates into another. The sins of youth expire, replaced by those of middle years, and then those of age. Some sins die a violent death, and some a natural: poverty, imprisonment, banishment may kill some sins, while others die of age as we become less able to commit them. For example, immorality takes on new life as ambition, followed by spiritual coldness.

This cycle of sin causes me to fear a relapse, O God, especially because I have had multiple relapses already. What makes a relapse so odious to you? With Israel, it was not so much their murmuring and idolatry but their repetitions of those sins that seemed to affect you. *How often they rebelled against him in the wilderness and grieved him in the wasteland! Again and again they put God to the test; they vexed the Holy One of Israel* (Psalm 78:40-41). For this reason you vowed not to leave them unpunished.

Whoever sins and then repents has weighed God and the devil in a balance and chosen the right path; but if we return to sin, we decide for Satan, choosing sin over grace and Satan before God. In short, we stand in contempt of God, and such contempt wounds deeper than an injury, a relapse deeper than a blasphemy.

After you have told me that a relapse is more odious to you, need I ask what makes it dangerous to me? What danger could be greater than provoking your displeasure? My sickness brought me to you in repentance and my relapse has cast me further from you. *Stop sinning or something worse may happen to you*, your Son told a man whom he had healed (John 5:14). That's the danger I face: death may be an end worse than sickness, but hell is the beginning of an end even worse.

Your disciple Peter denied your Son three times, but each took place before his repentance; afterward he did not relapse. O, if you had ever readmitted Adam into Paradise, how guardedly would he have walked past that tree! And wouldn't the angels that fell have fixed themselves upon you, if you had once admitted them to your sight?

Should I relapse, won't my case be just as desperate? No, not so desperate, for your mercy equals your majesty. You, who have commanded me to forgive my brother seventy-seven times, have limited yourself to no number. If your mercy in pardoning might lead to a relapse for which there was no further forgiveness, we'd be worse off than before. Who can avoid sinning while on earth? I say this, O my God, not to prepare a way to my relapse, but to stave off a sense of desperation if a relapse does indeed occur.

PRAYER

O ETERNAL AND MOST GRACIOUS GOD, you invite us to approach you in prayer and bring our petitions to you. So now I come to you with two requests. I have meditated on your honor, and concluded that nothing comes nearer to violating that honor than to beg for your forgiveness, receive it, and then return to the sin that prompted my request. That resembles a kind of spiritual fornication.

Your correction has brought me to a state of union with you. O my God, the God of constancy and perseverance, preserve me in this state from all relapses into those sins that you have corrected, and then forgiven.

Because I know my slippery self all too well, I presume to add this petition too: that you not forsake me if my infirmity overtakes me. Say to my soul, *My son, you have sinned; do so no more.* But say also that, even if I do, your spirit of remorse and conviction shall never depart from me.

Your holy apostle, St. Paul, endured three shipwrecks and still was saved. Though the rocks and the sands, the heights and the shallows, the prosperity and the adversity of this world, do threaten me, and though my own leaky soul endanger me, may I *hold on to faith and a good conscience*, and not join those who *have rejected and so have suffered shipwreck with regard to the faith* (1 Timothy 1:19).

Then your everlasting mercy will shelter me, even if what I most earnestly pray against might befall me, a relapse into those sins which I have truly repented, and you have fully pardoned.

26

DEATH DEFANGED

(PHILIP YANCEY)

*Though so disobedient a servant as I may be afraid to die, yet
to so merciful a master as thou I cannot be afraid to come.*

Two great crises spawned by Donne's illness, the crisis of fear
and the crisis of meaning, converged in a third and final crisis:
death. "I tune my instrument here at the door," he wrote—
the door of death. The poet truly believed that he would die
from his illness, and that dark cloud hangs over every page
of *Devotions*.

We moderns have perfected techniques for coping with
this crisis, techniques that doubtless would cause John Donne
much puzzlement. Most of us construct elaborate means
of avoiding death altogether. Fitness clubs are a booming
industry, as are nutrition and health food stores. We treat
physical health like a religion, while simultaneously walling
off death's blunt reminders: mortuaries, intensive care units,
cemeteries. Living in plague times, Donne did not have
the luxury of denial. Each night horse-drawn carts rum-
bled through the streets to collect the bodies of that day's
victims; their names—over a thousand each day at the
plague's height—appeared in long columns in the next day's

newspaper. No one could live as though death did not exist. Like others from his time, Donne kept a skull on his desk as a reminder, *memento mori*.

On the other hand, some modern health workers have taken the opposite tack, recommending acceptance, not denial, as the ideal attitude toward death. After Elisabeth Kübler-Ross labeled acceptance the final stage in the grief process, scores of groups sprang up to help terminally ill patients attain that stage. One need not read far in John Donne's work to realize how foreign such an idea might seem to him. Some have accused Donne of an obsession with death (thirty-two of his fifty-four songs and sonnets center on the theme), but for Donne death loomed as the great enemy to be resisted, not a friend to be welcomed as a natural part of life's cycle. From the times that I have watched, week by week, a friend or loved one deteriorate, I too know death as an enemy.

Donne's journal records an active struggle against accepting death. Despite his best efforts, he could not really imagine an afterlife. The pleasures that he knew so well, that filled his writings, all depended on his physical body and its ability to smell and see and hear and touch and taste.

Pastorally, Donne took some comfort in the example of Jesus, "my master in the science of death," as the account of the Garden of Gethsemane hardly presents a scene of calm acceptance either. There, Jesus sweat drops of blood and begged the Father for some other way. He too felt the kind of loneliness and fear that haunted Donne's sickbed. And why had he chosen that death? The purpose of Christ's death brought Donne some solace at last: he had died in order to effect a cure.

A turning point came for Donne as he began to view

death not as the disease that permanently spoils life, rather as the only cure to the disease of life, the final stage in the journey that brings us to God. Evil infects all of life on this fallen planet; only through death—Christ's death and our own—can we realize a resurrected state that restores us, uniting body and soul. Donne explored that thought in "A Hymn to God the Father," the only other writing known to survive from his time of illness:

Wilt thou forgive that sin where I begun,
Which was my sin, though it were done before?
Wilt thou forgive that sin, through which I run,
    And do run still: though still I do deplore?
        When thou hast done, thou hast not done,
            For, I have more.

Wilt thou forgive that sin which I have won
    Others to sin? and, made my sin their door?
Wilt thou forgive that sin which I did shun
    A year, or two: but wallowed in, a score?
        When thou hast done, thou hast not done,
            For I have more.

I have a sin of fear, that when I have spun
    My last thread, I shall perish on the shore;
But swear by thy self, that at my death thy son
    Shall shine as he shines now, and heretofore;
        And, having done that, thou hast done,
            I fear no more.

The word-play on the poet's name ("thou hast *done*") reveals a kind of acceptance at last: not an acceptance of death as a natural end, but a willingness to trust God with the future, no matter what. "That voice, that I must die now, is not the voice of a judge that speaks by way of condemnation, but of a physician that presents health."

⌐⌐

As it happened, to everyone's astonishment John Donne did not die from the illness of 1623. His illness, misdiagnosed, proved to be a spotted fever like typhus, not bubonic plague. He survived the physicians' bizarre treatments, recovered, and served for eight more years as Dean of St. Paul's Cathedral.

Donne's later sermons and writings often returned to the themes touched upon in *Devotions*, especially the theme of death, yet never again did they express the same sort of inner turmoil. In his crisis, Donne managed to achieve a "holy indifference" to death: not by a discounting of death's horror—his later sermons contain vivid depictions of those horrors—but rather by a renewed confidence in resurrection. Death, which appears to sever life, actually opens a door to new life. "O death, where is thy sting? O grave, where is thy victory?"

If Donne could somehow time-travel into modern times, he would no doubt be aghast at how little attention we give to the afterlife. Today, people are almost embarrassed to talk about such a belief. We fear heaven as our ancestors feared hell. The notion seems quaint, cowardly, an escape from this world's problems. What inversion of values, I wonder, has led us to commend a belief in no afterlife as brave, and dismiss a hope for blissful eternity as cowardly? Heaven holds out a promise of a time, far longer and more substantial than this time on earth, of wholeness and justice and pleasure and peace. If we do not believe that, then, as the apostle Paul argued in 1 Corinthians 15, there's little reason for being a Christian in the first place. If we do believe, it should change our lives, as it changed John Donne's.

God knows all this world's weight and burden and heaviness, said Donne in a sermon; "And if there were not a weight of future glory to counterpoise it, we should all sink into nothing."

> Death be not proud, though some have called thee
> Mighty and dreadful, for, thou art not so . . .
> . . . One short sleep past, we wake eternally,
> And death shall be no more, Death thou shalt die.

27

The Peace of Acceptance

(Philip Yancey)

There I shall be all light, no shadow upon me.

Seven years after the illness that inspired *Devotions*, Donne suffered another illness, which would severely test all that he had learned about pain. He spent most of the winter of 1630 out of the pulpit, confined to a house in Essex. But when the time of the Passion approached on the church calendar, Donne insisted on traveling to London to deliver a sermon on the first Friday of Lent. The friends who greeted him there saw an emaciated man, looking much older than his fifty-eight years. A lifetime of suffering had taken its toll. Although friends urged Donne to cancel the scheduled sermon, he refused.

Donne's first biographer, his contemporary Izaac Walton, sets the scene at Whitehall Palace on the day of Donne's last sermon:

> Doubtless many did secretly ask that question in Ezekiel, "Do these bones live?" Or can that soul organise that tongue? . . . Doubtless it cannot. And yet, after some faint pauses in his zealous prayer, his strong desires enabled his weak body to discharge his memory of his preconceived

meditations, which were of dying; the text being, "To God the Lord belong the issues from death." Many that then saw his tears, and heard his faint and hollow voice, professing they thought the text prophetically chosen, and that Dr. Donne had preached his own Funeral Sermon. (From *The Life of Dr. John Donne*)

Donne had often expressed the desire to die in the pulpit, and so he nearly did. The impact of that sermon, "Death's Duel," one of Donne's finest, did not soon fade from those who heard it. To John Donne, death was an enemy he would fight as long as strength remained in his bones. He fought with the confident faith that the enemy would ultimately be defeated.

Carried to his house, Donne spent the next five weeks preparing for his death. He dictated letters to friends, wrote a few poems, and composed his own epitaph. Acquaintances dropped by, and he reminisced. "I cannot plead innocency of life, especially of my youth," he told one friend, "but I am to be judged by a merciful God, who is not willing to see what I have done amiss. And though of myself I have nothing to present to Him but sins and misery, yet I know He looks upon me not as I am of myself, but as I am in my Savior . . . I am therefore full of inexpressible joy, and shall die in peace."

Izaac Walton contrasted the image of John Donne in those final days—his body gaunt and wasted but his spirit at rest—with a portrait he had seen of Donne at age eighteen, as a dashing young cavalier, bedecked in finery, brandishing a sword. Its inscription, notes Walton, had proved ironically prophetic of Donne's difficult life: "How much shall I be changed before I am changed!"

A carver came by during those last few weeks, under orders from the church to design a monument. Donne posed for him in the posture of death, a winding sheet wrapped around him, his hands folded over his stomach, his eyes closed. The effigy was carved out of a single piece of white marble, and after Donne's death workmen mounted it over his funeral urn in St. Paul's Cathedral.

It is still there, John Donne's monument. It was, in fact, the only object in St. Paul's to survive the Great Fire of 1666, and it can be viewed in the ambulatory of the cathedral rebuilt by Christopher Wren, behind the choir stalls, an ivory-colored monument set in a niche in the old gray stone. Tour guides point out a brown scorch mark on the urn dating from the fire. Donne's face wears an expression of serenity, as though he attained at last in death the peace that eluded him for so much of life.

> Our last day is our first day; our Saturday is our Sunday; our eve is our holy day; our sunsetting is our morning; the day of our death is the first day of our eternal life. The next day after that . . . comes that day that shall show me to myself. Here I never saw myself but in disguises; there, then, I shall see myself, but I shall see God too. . . . Here I have one faculty enlightened, and another left in darkness; mine understanding sometimes cleared, my will at the same time perverted. There I shall be all light, no shadow upon me; my soul invested in the light of joy, and my body in the light of glory. (From Donne's *Sermons*)

⌒

Another monument lives on in Donne's writings. I have read many words on the problem of pain, and written some myself. Nowhere, however, have I found such a concentrated, wise meditation on the human condition as in the journal John Donne kept during the weeks of his illness, as he lay preparing for death. Having braced himself to wrestle with God, he instead found himself in the arms of a merciful Physician, who tenderly guided him through the crisis so that he could emerge to give comfort and hope to others.

The apostle Paul, imprisoned and unsure whether he would survive to get out of jail or meet death by execution, told the Philippians that either way he was content.

> For I know that through your prayers and God's provision of the Spirit of Jesus Christ what has happened to me will turn out for my deliverance. I eagerly expect and hope that I will in no way be ashamed, but will have sufficient courage so that now as always Christ will be exalted in my body, whether by life or by death. For to me, to live is Christ and to die is gain. (Philippians 1:19-21)

Donne finally experienced peace before he died, replacing dread and anxiety. He was following the path of Paul who, not knowing whether he faced life or death, modeled an equanimity rooted in his trust in God. Either way, God would be with him.

Their insights can help us find our own way through the whiplash of emotions that crisis puts us through. When the next moment pushes us toward resignation and dread, can we choose to discover acceptance and even joy?

⁓

As a writer who works at home, I am well acquainted with solitude, though not the kind of social isolation imposed during the coronavirus's outbreak. When my state of Colorado first issued a stay-at-home order in 2020, I realized that like most Americans I was spending too much time listening to news reports of body counts and the relentless progress of COVID-19. Early on, feeling disconnected from the rapidly changing world outside, I had filled every moment with news reports and podcasts, as if sending out feelers to remind myself I was still part of humanity and shared its plight.

Eventually I felt burdened by the constant reminders of events over which I had no control, and decided instead to unplug. For relief, and with fitness centers closed, I began taking long hikes in the Rocky Mountains. I started reading poetry, mostly W. H. Auden and Mary Oliver, and adjusted to the slower, quieter pace that poetry demands.

That weekend, a spring snowstorm fell in the foothills. My wife and I walked for an hour through untracked snow, breathing the mountain air and kicking out a trail under evergreens blanketed in pure white. I needed that break, shielded from the tiresome cycle of negative news, and I embraced the reminder that, for all its problems, the earth we inhabit is a place of indescribable beauty.

Steven Garber writes, in his book *Visions of Vocation*:

As the poet Bob Dylan once sang, Everything is broken. Yes, everything, and so we must not be romantics. We cannot afford to be, just as we cannot be stoics or cynics either.

But the story of sorrow is not the whole story of life either. There is also wonder and glory, joy and meaning, in the vocations that are ours. There is good work to be done by every son of Adam and every daughter of Eve all over the face of the earth. There are flowers to be grown, songs to be sung, bread to be baked, justice to be done, mercy to be shown, beauty to be created, good stories to be told, houses to be built, technologies to be developed, fields to farm, and children to educate.

All day, every day, there are both wounds and wonders at the very heart of life, if we have eyes to see.

28

Finding Meaning in Suffering

(Philip Yancey)

Make this . . . very dejection and faintness of heart, a
powerful cordial.

Viktor Frankl, survivor of a Nazi concentration camp, iden-
tified another great crisis faced by people who suffer: the
crisis of meaning. "Despair," he said, "is suffering without
meaning." He had observed that fellow inmates could endure
severe suffering as long as they had some hope in its redemp-
tive value. In a very different society such as ours, saturated
with comfort, what possible meaning can we give to the great
intruder, pain?

I have an entire bookcase on the topic of pain and suffering. During COVID quarantine I spent hours thumbing
through those I had marked and highlighted over the years.
Unanswered questions—the planet's future, God's involve-
ment in pandemics, the randomness of who gets sick and who
stays healthy—still swirled around. More and more, though,
as I read accounts of suffering, they reduced down to a single
person honestly confronting pain and mortality in the presence of God.

In his classic book *The Problem of Pain*, C. S. Lewis

answered convincingly many of the questions that arise when we suffer. But years later Lewis's wife, Joy, contracted cancer. He watched her wither away and die in a hospital bed. Subsequently he wrote another, far more personal and emotional, book on pain. In that account, *A Grief Observed*, Lewis writes:

> Meanwhile, where is God? This is one of the most disquieting symptoms. When you are happy, so happy that you have no sense of needing Him, if you turn to Him then with praise, you will be welcomed with open arms. But go to Him when your need is desperate, when all other help is vain and what do you find? A door slammed in your face, and a sound of bolting and double bolting on the inside. After that, silence. You may as well turn away.

In the end, as Lewis found, suffering is not a problem to be solved but a burden to be borne. We are reduced to bewildered, mortal creatures facing existential questions for which we have no satisfying answer.

In John Donne's day, it seemed that God's molten wrath was showering down on the entire planet. Two bright comets appeared in the sky each night—sure signs, said some, of God's hand behind the plague. Prophets roamed the streets, one echoing Jonah with his cry, "Yet forty days and London shall be destroyed!" Theologians in Europe debated for four centuries God's message in the Great Plague, yet in the end a little rat poison silenced all their speculation.

What about the meaning of progeria, the tragic abnormality that speeds up the aging process and causes a six-year-old child to look and feel eighty? Or what is the meaning of cerebral palsy, or cystic fibrosis? What is the meaning of an earthquake in Turkey, or a freak tidal wave that kills a hundred thousand people in Bangladesh? Why does a Colorado wildfire destroy one house and skip right over the neighbors' houses? What is the meaning of terminal cancer? Or bubonic plague?

Early in my diagnosis of Parkinson's Disease, I sat in the waiting room of a neurology clinic and looked around me at people with "movement disorders," a group of ailments that disrupt connections between muscles and the brain. Parkinson's patients vary widely, from some with mild tremors to others who must lean on a walker or use a wheelchair. Others who suffer from Lewy body dementia, Huntington's disease, or ALS face the certain knowledge of worsening symptoms, leading to death. I have written books about the wonders of the human body. What purpose can these debilitating diseases serve?

John Donne contemplated related questions as he lay gravely ill. He feared not only death, but the terror of a long, painful decline. How can that be meaningful? In a letter to a widowed friend, he wrote "I am afraid that Death will play with me so long, as he will forget to kill me, and suffer me to live in a languishing and useless age."

Through the open window of his bedroom, Donne heard church bells tolling out a doleful declaration of death. For an instant he wondered if his friends, knowing his condition to be more grave than they had disclosed, had ordered the bells rung for his own death. He soon realized that they were marking another person's death, one more victim of the plague.

A short time later, sounds from the funeral service drifted in among the street noises. Donne croaked out a feeble accompaniment to the congregational singing of psalms, and that's when he wrote the meditation and reflection on the meaning of the church bells—the most famous portion of *Devotions*, and one of the most celebrated passages in English literature: "No man is an island . . . if a clod be washed away by the sea, Europe is the less . . . any man's death diminishes me, because I am involved in mankind, and therefore never send to know for whom the bell tolls; it tolls for thee." We grieve at another's death because we ourselves are diminished. In the same event we sense a deep unity with others, and also its rending.

The tolling of that bell worked a curious twist in Donne's thinking. To that point, he had been wondering about the meaning of illness and what lessons to learn from it. Now he began contemplating the meaning of health. The bell called into question how he had spent his entire life. Had he hallowed the gift of health by serving others and God? Had he viewed life as a preparation, a training ground, for a far longer and more important life to come—or as an end in itself?

As Donne began to reexamine his life, surprises came to light. It now seemed clear that his times of affliction, the circumstances he most resented at the time, turned out to be the very occasions of spiritual growth. Trials had purged sin and developed character; poverty had taught him dependence on God and cleansed him of greed; failure and public disgrace had helped cure pride and ambition. A definite pattern emerged: pain could be transformed, even redeemed, and apparent evil sometimes results in actual good. Suffering not removed may serve as God's tool.

Donne's systematic review brought him up to his present circumstances. Could even *this* pain be redeemed? His illness limited him, of course, but the physical incapacity surely did not inhibit all spiritual growth. He had much time for prayer: the bell had reminded him of his less fortunate neighbor, and the many others afflicted in London. He could learn humility, and trust, and gratitude, and faith.

Donne made a kind of game of it: he envisioned his soul growing strong, rising from the bed, and walking about the room even as his body lay flat. He directed his energy toward spiritual disciplines: prayer, confession of sins, keeping a journal (which became *Devotions*). He got his mind off himself and onto others.

The meditations included in *Devotions* thus record a crucial shift in Donne's attitude toward pain. He began with prayers that the pain be removed; he ends with prayers that the pain be redeemed, that he be "catechized by affliction." Such redemption might take the form of miraculous cure—he still hoped so—but even if it did not, God could take a crude lump and through the refiner's fire of suffering make of it pure gold.

29

COMPASSION, NOT BLAME

(PHILIP YANCEY)

Give me tender and supple and conformable affections,
that as I joy with them that joy, and mourn with them that
mourn, so I may fear with them that fear.

IN SEPTEMBER 2013, a creek outside my home rose nearly
six feet in a "flood of the century" and came within inches of
overflowing its banks and flooding my office. I spent the next
day filling sandbags and placing them against the eroding
bank. Whole trees and bridges hurtled past me, and if I didn't
position a forty-pound sandbag just right, the creek would
grab it and whisk it away like a piece of litter.

Exhausted, soaked, covered with mud, I came inside to
clean up, only to hear a pastor from Colorado Springs pontif-
icate that the flood of the century was occurring because our
state legislature had recently legalized gay marriage and mari-
juana. I shook my head in dismay over another self-appointed
prophet attempting to speak for God.

In early 2020, during the initial onslaught in the U.S.
of COVID-19, I wondered what that same pastor would say
about the thirty-three African-American bishops and denom-
inational leaders around the country who died from the virus.

Or about the members of a small church in Calgary, Canada, who gathered to celebrate the birthday of one of their most beloved senior citizens and followed strict protocol, limiting the gathering to less than fifty and maintaining a six-foot social distance—yet twenty-four of the forty-one who attended contracted the virus, and two died.

I sometimes wish that pastors and other Christian spokespersons would take a variation of the Hippocratic oath, beginning with the promise to "Do no harm." Almost by instinct, we respond to suffering as a kind of karmic punishment. *We* [or they] *must have done something wrong. God is trying to tell us something.* It's one thing to use a tragedy as a time to pause and reflect on what needs changing, and quite another to piously blame the victims for bringing about that tragedy.

In the specific case of the novel coronavirus, questions of causation are best left in the hands of scientists, not pastors or amateur theologians. Viruses and bacteria are the most abundant and diverse beings on earth, most of them beneficial, but some of them do mutate and cause problems for the human immune system. Clearly, God has not chosen to intervene with every new virus mutation, every thunderstorm, every shifting of tectonic plates.

We live on an imperfect, broken planet that displeases God as much as it displeases us. Jesus asked us to pray that God's will "be done on earth as it is in heaven," and that prayer has not yet been answered on planet earth. In the words of the apostle Paul, "the whole creation has been groaning as in the pains of childbirth right up to the present time" (Romans 8:22).

There's an easy correction to the reflex response of assuming tragedy comes as God's punishment. Simply follow

Jesus through the Gospels and watch his response to a person afflicted with leprosy, a blind beggar by the road, or even a Roman officer whose servant has fallen ill. Always, without exception, he responds with comfort and healing. Never does he blame the victim or philosophize about the cause. If we want to know how God feels about people who are suffering—from poverty, oppression, cancer, or a pandemic—all we need do is look at Jesus' compassionate response. God is on their side.

⌒

Compassion should ultimately lead to action. In *Dominion: How the Christian Revolution Remade the World,* British historian Tom Holland documents how members of the early church cared for the poor and dying and adopted abandoned babies. Sociologist Rodney Stark (*The Rise of Christianity*) observes that one reason the church grew so rapidly within the Roman Empire traces back to how Christians responded to pandemics of the day, which probably included smallpox and bubonic plague. When infection spread, Romans fled their cities and towns; Christians stayed behind to nurse and feed not only their own relatives but also their pagan neighbors.

During a podcast conversation, the President of Denver Seminary, Mark Young, told me of a seminary graduate who worked as a chaplain in a facility for seniors with dementia. The facility had banned all visitors, and as a result fourteen times the chaplain had been the sole person sitting with a resident as he or she died. Fourteen times she had to go outside the quarantine area and meet with the families of the deceased, who were anxious to know all the agonizing details.

"Where is God in a situation like that?" Mark asked. Of course, he knew the answer. God was present in that chaplain who brought comfort as best she could, first to the dying person and then to the family left behind.

When Jesus ascended, he sent his followers into the world "as the Father has sent me," to carry on his mission of comfort and healing. In a lovely phrase, the apostle Paul refers to God as *the Father of compassion and the God of all comfort*, "who comforts us in all our troubles, so that we can comfort those in any trouble with the comfort we ourselves receive from God" (2 Corinthians 1:3-4). That is the Christian's stated mission in a world full of pain and suffering. Theologian Stanley Hauerwas once described the church as "a company of people who have learned how to be ill and to ask for help and how to be present to one another in and out of pain."

⌇

A friend who heard the news about my diagnosis of Parkinson's Disease sent me a reference to Psalm 71, which leads with these words:

> In you, Lord, I have taken refuge;
>> let me never be put to shame.

Although the psalmist wrote in very different circumstances, harassed by human enemies rather than a nerve disease, the words "let me never be put to shame" jumped out at me. Other psalms (see 25, 31, and 34) repeat the odd phrase.

A measure of shame seems to accompany disability or illness, and Donne described that shame in *Devotions*. An innate shame in inconveniencing others for something that is neither your fault nor your desire. A paranoia in knowing friends (or doctors) are making decisions about you behind your back. The indignity of needing help with simple activities like taking a bath and getting dressed. And a shame in having well-meaning friends overreact: some may treat you like a fragile antique, or complete your sentences when you pause a second to think of a word.

Though still experiencing only mild symptoms, already I anticipate shame over how these may worsen: drooling, memory gaps, slurred speech, sudden falls, uncontrolled tremors.

After my diagnosis, six friends wrote that they had observed something unsound about me, but didn't mention it. Only two risked being as blatantly honest as a child. During a restaurant dinner one said to me, "Have you got the slows, Philip?"—earning a look of reproof from his wife. Another, more blunt, asked, "Why are you walking like a decrepit old man?" Those two comments spurred me to intensify my search for a neurologist. Shame can sometimes goad to action.

"Do not cast me away when I am old; do not forsake me when my strength is gone," Psalm 71 adds. That prayer expresses the silent plea of all disabled persons, a group that now includes me. The CDC calculates that a fourth of the U.S. population qualifies as disabled. Now that I have joined them, I try to look past the externals to the person inside.

As I informed a few close friends, I feared that now I

had acquired a new label: not just *Philip* but *Philip-with-Parkinson's*. That's how people would see me, think of me, and talk about me. I want to insist, "I'm still the same person inside, so please don't judge me by externals such as slowness, stumbling, and occasional tremors." In fact, I coined a new word—*dislabled*—in protest.

A newly vocal generation wears the *disabled* label as a badge of honor. Some members of the deaf community, for example, scorn such euphemisms as "hearing impaired" and refuse medical procedures that might restore their hearing. In contrast, I admit I would be delighted to have Parkinson's magically removed from my life. I would hold a pill bonfire, cancel my order for a cane, and dust off my mountain climbing gear. However, I don't have that option, and perhaps the disability activists are simply focusing on accepting the reality that some things can't be changed.

⌒

My own "disability" has altered how I view others. On a recent airplane trip, I sat in the row just behind first class, in the economy section. The elderly first-class passenger ahead of me clogged up the entire disembarking procedure. He needed help getting his carryon luggage from the overhead compartment, stumbled and sat down a few times, and stood in the aisle to catch his breath, blocking all the rest of us from moving. Passengers behind me were loudly grumbling about the inconvenience. I thought, *That could be me in a few years. Is that my future?* If so, how will I handle it?

In my writing career I have interviewed U.S. presidents,

rock stars, professional athletes, actors, and other celebrities. I have also profiled leprosy patients in India, pastors imprisoned for their faith in China, women rescued from sexual trafficking, parents of children with rare genetic disorders, and many who suffer from diseases more debilitating than Parkinson's. As I reflect on the two groups, here's what stands out: with some exceptions, those who live with pain and failure tend to be better stewards of their life circumstances than those who live with success and pleasure. Pain redeemed impresses me more than pain removed.

This latest twist in my own life involves a disease that could prove incapacitating or perhaps a mere inconvenience; Parkinson's has a wide spectrum of manifestations. How should I prepare? I was blessed to know Michael Gerson, a *New York Times* columnist and White House speech-writer who lived with Parkinson's for years before succumbing to cancer. A colleague said of him, "At the peak of his career, he used his influence to care for the most vulnerable, spearheading the campaign to address AIDS in Africa. When he was at his lowest point physically, he never complained but focused on gratitude for the life he had lived."

That is my prayerful goal. After a bumpy childhood, I've had a rich, full, and wonderful life with more pleasure and fulfillment than I ever dreamed of or deserved. I have an omni-competent wife of more than 50 years who takes my health and well-being as a personal challenge. Sixteen years ago, when I lay strapped to a backboard with a broken neck after an auto accident, Janet drove through a blizzard to retrieve me. Already she was mentally re-designing our house in case she needed to prepare for life with a paralytic. She shows that same selfless, fierce loyalty now, even as she faces the potentially demanding role of caregiver.

My future is full of question marks, and I'm not unduly anxious. I have excellent medical care and support from friends. I trust a good and loving God who often chooses to reveal those qualities through his followers on earth. I have written many words on suffering, and now am being called to put them into practice. May I, like Michael Gerson, like John Donne, be a faithful steward of this latest chapter.

30

FROM FEAR TO TRUST

(PHILIP YANCEY)

Give me, O Lord, a fear, of which I may not be afraid.

Every time I open the doors of a hospital and breathe in its familiar antiseptic odor, I clench in fear, even as a visitor. The sterile surroundings conjure up the loneliness of lying in a medical bed feeling miserable, interrupted only by the poking and prodding of tests while nurses and doctors confer among themselves in lowered voices.

John Donne likewise described the disconnected sensation that moves in when doctors hover over a patient. When he sensed fear in the physician, his own fears bubbled to the surface: "I overtake him, I overrun him, in his fear." As a patient, he felt like an object, like a map spread out across a table, pored over by cosmographers. He imagined himself separated from his own body and floating above it, from which vantage he could observe the disintegrating figure on the bed. As the illness advanced, he saw himself as a statue of clay, its limbs and flesh melting off and crumbling into a handful of sand. Soon nothing would remain save a pile of bones.

Most of the time Donne had to battle such fears alone, for

in those days doctors quarantined patients with contagious diseases, posting a warning notice on their doors. As Donne lay inside he wondered if God, too, was participating in the quarantine. He cried out, but received no answer. Where was God's promised presence? His comfort? In each of the twenty-three meditations, Donne circles back to the main issue underlying his suffering. His real fear was not the tinny clamor of pain cells all over his body; he feared God.

Calvinism was still new then, with its emphasis on God's absolute sovereignty, and Donne pondered the notion of plagues and wars as "God's angels." He soon recoiled: "Surely it is not thou, it is not thy hand. The devouring sword, the consuming fire, the winds from the wilderness, the diseases of the body, all that afflicted Job, were from the hands of Satan; it is not thou." Yet he never felt certain, and the not knowing caused much inner torment. Guilt from his spotted past lurked nearby, like a leering demon. Perhaps he was indeed suffering as a result of sin. And if so, was it better to be scarred by God, or not visited at all? How could he worship, let alone love, such a God?

⌒

Although *Devotions* does not answer the philosophical questions, it does record Donne's emotional resolution, a gradual movement toward peace. At first—confined to bed, churning out prayers without answers, contemplating death, regurgitating guilt—he can find no relief from fear. Obsessed, he reviews every biblical occurrence of the word *fear*. As he does so, it dawns on him that life will always include circumstances that incite fear: if not illness, financial hardship; if not poverty, rejection; if not loneliness, failure. In such a world, Donne has a choice: to fear God, or to fear everything else.

In a passage reminiscent of Paul's litany in Romans 8 ("For I am convinced that neither death nor life . . . will be able to separate us from the love of God . . ."), Donne checks off his potential fears. Personal enemies pose no ultimate threat, for God can vanquish any enemy. Famine? No, for God can supply. Death? Even that, the worst human fear, offers no final barrier against God's love. Donne concludes his best course is to cultivate a proper fear of the Lord, a fear which can supplant all others: "as thou hast given me a repentance, not to be repented of, so give me, O Lord, a fear, of which I may not be afraid." I learned from Donne, when faced with doubts, to review my alternatives. If for whatever reason I refuse to trust God, what, then, can I trust?

In his disputation with God, Donne has changed questions. He began with the question of *cause*—"Who caused this illness, this plague? And why?"—for which he found no answer. The meditations move ever so gradually toward the question of *response*, the defining issue that confronts every person who suffers. Will I trust God with my crisis, and the fear it provokes? Or will I turn away from God in bitterness and anger? Donne decided that in the most important sense it did not matter whether his sickness was a chastening or merely a natural occurrence. In either case he would trust God, for in the end *trust* represents the proper fear of the Lord.

Donne likened the process to his changing attitude toward physicians. Initially, as they probed his body for new symptoms and discussed their findings in hushed tones outside his room, he could not help feeling afraid. In time, however, sensing their compassionate concern, he became convinced that they deserved his trust. The same pattern applies to God. We often do not understand God's methods or the reasons behind them. The most important question, though, is whether God is a trustworthy "physician." Donne concluded yes.

Many people do not envision a God worthy of trust. From the church, they hear mostly condemnation. That is why, following Donne, I turn for perspective to the central reason for trusting God: because in Jesus, God gave us a face.

To learn how God views suffering on this planet, we need only look at the face of Jesus as he moves among paralytics, widows, and those with leprosy. In contrast to others in his day, Jesus showed an unusual tenderness toward those whom others thought deserved their fate. In Jesus, said Donne, we have a Great Physician "who knows our natural infirmities, for he had them, and knows the weight of our sins, for he paid a dear price for them."

How can we approach a God we fear? In answer, Donne holds up a phrase from Matthew's story of the women who discovered the empty tomb after Jesus' resurrection. They hurried away from the scene "with fear and yet great joy," and Donne saw in their "two legs of fear and joy" a pattern for himself. Those women had seen with their own eyes the vast distance between immortal God and mortal man, but suddenly it was a distance to inspire joy. God had used his great power to conquer the last enemy, death. For that reason, the women felt both fear and great joy. And for that reason, John Donne found at last a fear of which he need not be afraid.

In 2020, Easter Sunday fell at a time when COVID-19 was ravaging the country, and most churches had to resort to technology, live-streaming their services from eerily empty buildings. Hope seemed almost as elusive as it must have been to the disciples who watched their leader die. But the three-day pattern—Friday's tragedy, Saturday's despair, Sunday's triumph—became for Jesus' followers a pattern that can be applied to all our times of tribulation.

Good Friday demonstrates that God is not indifferent to our pain; God, too, is personally "acquainted with grief." Holy Saturday hints that we may go through seasons of confusion and seeming defeat. And Easter Sunday shows that, in the end, suffering will not prevail.

O God, you bring death and give life.
Whatever comes, comes from you;
no matter what comes,
let me come to you.